Contents

Introduction

The importance of numeracy

There are few people in our society who would not subscribe to the view that numeracy is an essential life-skill and so should be afforded great importance at all levels of education. This is particularly true in the early years, indeed it should be the right of every child to become numerate by the time they leave primary school. It is therefore absolutely correct that number work occupies a large proportion of time in the early years to such an extent that 'number' is often synonymous with 'mathematics'. However, it is important that too narrow a definition is not placed on 'number' or 'numeracy'. Both are concerned with much more than just basic arithmetic. Number work involves an understanding of the number system and place value, an awareness of the patterns and relationships which exist between numbers, as well as a knowledge of various computational skills. Finally, let us not forget that the whole purpose of learning about number is so that we can use and apply what we have learned. Children should therefore spend a large amount of time using and applying their number skills to solve problems, to handle data and to measure various aspects of the world around them. It is because number work reaches out into all of these areas that numeracy is such an important skill for life.

About this book

This book provides a bank of activities which are designed to help children to develop knowledge, skills and understanding in number. The activities can easily be incorporated into any existing mathematics scheme of work and can be used in conjunction with other published resources. They have been designed to support the Framework for Teaching Mathematics by incorporating several key features:

A strong emphasis on whole-class teaching: Every lesson starts with a whole-class, teacher-led introduction and concludes in the same way. The intention is that all pupils in the class will be doing mathematics at the same time, although during the main activity there is the opportunity for different groups of pupils to do slightly different tasks according to ability.

A strong emphasis on interactive teaching: The teacher plays a key role in every lesson and acts as much more than simply a facilitator or passive observer. The teacher is expected to interact with the pupils throughout the lesson, particularly when working with the whole class during the introduction and plenary. Here, the interaction is stimulated by asking appropriate questions to encourage the pupils to think about, explain and discuss mathematics. Every activity identifies key questions the teacher must ask to facilitate effective interaction with the pupils.

A strong emphasis on developing mental skills: Many activities focus on the development, reinforcement and practise of mental skills. Even if this is not the main focus, the interaction with pupils during the introduction and plenary is often used for quick-fire mental practice.

Lesson plans

The structure for each activity is as follows.

Activity title box

The box at the beginning of each activity outlines the following key aspects:

Learning objective

These learning objectives break down aspects of the programmes of study for Mathematics and the *Framework for Teaching Mathematics* into manageable teaching and learning chunks, and their purpose is to aid planning for progression. These objectives can easily be referenced to the National Curriculum and Scottish 5–14 requirements by using the overview grid on pages 7 to 13. The learning objectives are appropriately focused thus allowing judgements to be made about pupil progress at the end of each activity.

Class organization/Likely duration.

Icons ✝✝ and 🕐 signpost the suggested structure and group sizes for each activity and the approximate amount of time required to complete it. Nearly all of the activities begin with a whole-class introduction and conclude with a whole-class plenary but there is much variety in the organisation of the main part of the lesson.

Previous skills/knowledge needed

Information is given here when it is necessary for the children to have acquired specific knowledge or skills prior to carrying out the activity.

Key background information

This section outlines the areas of study covered by each activity and gives a general background to the particular topic or theme, outlining the basic skills that will be developed and the way in which the activity will address children's learning.

Preparation

Advice is given for those occasions when it is necessary for the teacher to prime the pupils for the activity or to prepare materials, or to set up a visual aid prior to the lesson.

Resources needed

All materials needed to carry out the activity are listed here.

What to do

Easy-to-follow, step-by-step instructions are given for carrying out the activity, including suggested questions for the teacher to ask pupils to help instigate discussion and stimulate investigation. These instructions are conveniently divided into three sections; introduction, main activity and plenary.

Suggestion(s) for extension/support

In these sections, suggestions are given for ways of providing differentiation.

Assessment opportunities

Where appropriate, opportunities for ongoing teacher assessment of the children's work during or after a specific activity are highlighted.

Opportunities for IT

Where opportunities for IT would strengthen an activity, these are briefly outlined with reference to particularly suitable types of program.

Display ideas

Where they are relevant and innovative, display ideas are incorporated into activity plans and illustrated with examples.

Reference to photocopiable sheets

Where activities include photocopiable activity sheets, small reproductions of these are included in the lesson plans together with guidance notes for their use and, where appropriate, suggested answers. Where appropriate, reference is also made to the photocopiable sheet in the *Preparation* section.

Overview Grid

This grid helps you to track the coverage of the Programme of Study for Maths at Key Stage One, or the Scottish National Guidelines for Mathematics 5–14 at Levels A–B, offered by the activities in this book. For each activity, the relevant statements from the National Curriculum for England and Wales and the Scottish 5–14 Guidelines are indicated (the latter references are given in italics).

Most of the activities in this book can be used alongside the activities in the *Curriculum Bank for Number at Key Stage One/Scottish Levels A–B*. These links are indicated by the notes in the shaded panel below the relevant activities. The National Numeracy Strategy (NNS) section in this grid shows how the activities relate to the key objectives set out in the Numeracy Framework. The page references refer to the supplement of examples, so that, for example, R p9 indicates Reception page 9.

ACTIVITY TITLE	LEARNING OBJECTIVE	POS/AO	NNS	CONTENT	PAGE
Giant calculator	To develop language associated with position such as 'next to', 'between', 'above', 'below'. To recognize numbers and mathematical symbols.	U&A 3a understand the language of number and comparatives N 2b read numbers up to 10. *Range and type of number level A*	Recognise numerals 1 to 9, extending to 0 (R p9). Use everyday words to describe position (R p27).	Pupils stick the keys onto a large poster-size reproduction of their calculator. Whole-class teacher-led practical activity.	14
Building 2-digit numbers, page 16;					
Calculator light-sticks	To be aware of the different ways that numbers can be drawn or displayed.	N 3e use a basic calculator, reading the display *As above, level A*	Recognise numerals 1 to 9, extending to 0 and 10, then beyond 10 (R p9). Begin to record numbers (R p10).	Discussion of how a calculator displays digits followed by a photocopiable sheet activity in which pupils record the digits. Individual photocopiable sheet-based activity.	15
Six light-sticks	To recognize and record numbers as they appear in an electronic display. To order one, two and three-digit numbers.	N 2b read, write and order numbers N 3e use a basic calculator, reading the display *As above, level A*	Read and write whole numbers to at least 100 (Y1/2 p8–9). Order whole numbers to at least 100 (Y1/2 p14–15).	Pupils find numbers which use exactly six light-sticks when displayed on a calculator and then arrange the numbers in order of size. Individual investigative activity.	17
Building 2-digit numbers, page 16; Largest number wins, page 18					
Calculator fishing	To recognize numbers when they are written in the style of an electronic display. To match the score on a dice shown as dots with the corresponding number in written form.	N 2a count up to 10 and beyond, knowing the number names N 2b read numbers up to 10 N 3e use a basic calculator, reading the display *As above, level A*	Recognise numerals 1 to 9 (R p9).	Pupils roll a dice and cover numbers on their own card. The numbers on the card are shown the way they appear on a calculator display. Bingo-type game played in small groups.	19
Match the animals, page 14					
Fast-fingers	To read, write and order one and two-digit numbers generated by a calculator. To develop and use correctly mathematical language associated with the size of numbers such as 'bigger than', 'smaller than', 'more than', 'less than', 'between'.	U&A 3a understand the language of number and comparatives N 2b read, write and order numbers N 3e use a basic calculator, reading the display *As above, level A*	Read and write numbers to at least 20 (Y1/2 p8–9). Understand and use the vocabulary of comparing and ordering numbers (Y1/2 p10–11). Order numbers to at least 20 (Y1/2 p14–15).	The constant function is used to turn a calculator into a counting machine. The numbers generated are used in ordering activities and to develop associated language. Calculator activity in small groups.	20
Largest number wins, page 18; Dotty numbers, page 20					

NUMBER SYSTEM AND PLACE VALUE

ACTIVITY TITLE	LEARNING OBJECTIVE	POS/AO	NNS	CONTENT	PAGE
Squeeze	To develop and correctly use mathematical language associated with the size of numbers for example 'bigger than', 'smaller than', 'more than', 'less than', 'between'. To identify a number which lies between two given numbers.	U&A 3a understand the language of number and comparatives N 2b read, write and order numbers *Range and type of number, level A*	Understand and use language to compare two numbers and say which is more and which is less (R p11). Say a number lying between two given numbers (R p12).	Pupils roll a dice twice and write down a number which lies between or exactly halfway between the two scores. Individual photocopiable sheet-based activity using a dice.	22
Boxes	To arrange numbers in order of size. To estimate where a number should come within a particular range.	N 2b order numbers *Range and type of number, level B*	Order whole numbers to at least 100 (Y1/2 p14–15) Understand and use the vocabulary of estimation (Y 1/2 p 16–17).	Pupils pick cards from a pack and judge the best place to put them so that all their numbers are in order at the end of the game. Estimating and ordering game played in pairs.	24
Largest number wins, page 18					
Guess the number	To use and understand mathematical language associated with size and order.	U&A 3a understand the language of number and comparatives U&A 3c respond to and ask mathematical questions *Range and type of number, level B*	Understand and use the vocabulary of comparing and ordering numbers (Y1/2 p16–17).	Pupils must identify an unknown number by asking questions which have a yes/no response. Game played in pairs.	26
Dotty numbers, page 20; Money money money, page 23					
Place value with HTU cards	To understand that the position of a digit affects its value.	N 2b develop an understanding that the position of a digit signifies its value. *Range and type of number, level B*	Know what each digit in a number represents (Y1/2 p8–9).	Pupils use a set of special cards to make numbers and then break these up into their constituent parts. Place value activity played in small groups.	27
Making numbers	To be able to make one, two and three-digit numbers from a list of digits provided. To order a set of one, two and three-digit numbers.	N 2b read, write and order numbers, developing an understanding that the position of a digit signifies its value. *As above, level B*	Read and write whole numbers to at least 100 (Y1/2 p8–9). Order whole numbers to at least 100 (Y1/2 p14–15).	Pupils make numbers from 3 digits and then order them. Individual activity.	29
Building 2-digit numbers, page 16					
Number flip-flaps	To generate numbers which fit certain criteria. To understand and correctly use mathematical language associated with the size and order of numbers.	U&A 3a understand the language of number and comparatives N 2b read, write and order numbers *As above, level B*	Read and write whole numbers to at least 100 (Y1/2 p8–9). Understand and use the vocabulary of comparing and ordering numbers (Y1/2 p10–11).	A simple piece of apparatus is used to generate 1 and 2-figure numbers which form the basis of sorting and ordering activities. Practical activity working individually.	31
Largest number wins, page 18					
Place value dice games	To understand that the position of a digit affects its value. To order a set of two-digit numbers.	N 2b read, write and order numbers, developing an understanding that the position of a digit signifies its value. *As above, level B*	Know what each digit in a number represents (Y1/2 p8–9). Order whole numbers to at least 100 (Y1/2 p14–15).	Pupils use a dice to generate two and three-digit numbers. Aim is to make the biggest number from the dice scores. Dice game played in pairs.	32

NUMBER KEY STAGE ONE

	ACTIVITY TITLE	LEARNING OBJECTIVE	POS/AO	NNS	CONTENT	PAGE
NUMBER RELATIONSHIPS	**Shade half**	To understand what is meant by 'half'. To shade half of a square in several different ways.	N 2c recognise and use in context simple fractions, including halves *Range and type of number, level A*	Recognise and find simple fractions (Y1/2 p20–21).	Pupils find as many ways as possible of shading half of a square. Individual activity.	34
	Fractions with pattern blocks	To understand what is meant by 'half'. To identify amounts that are more than or less than a half.	N 2c recognise and use in context simple fractions, including halves *As above, level A*	Recognise and find simple fractions (Y1/2 p20–21).	A shape-filling activity using pattern blocks in which pupils must shade less than half, exactly half and more than half. Individual photocopiable sheet activity using pattern blocks.	35

Equal parts, page 26; Matching halves, page 27; Partitioning sets, page 28; Sharing between three, page 29; Finding more fractions, page 31

	ACTIVITY TITLE	LEARNING OBJECTIVE	POS/AO	NNS	CONTENT	PAGE
	Repeating patterns	To understand what is meant by the expression 'repeating pattern'. To recognize and continue a repeating pattern using practical apparatus. To draw a repeating pattern.	U&A 4a recognise simple patterns N 3a use repeating patterns to develop ideas of regularity and sequencing *Patterns and sequences, level A*		Pupils continue a repeating pattern made from multilink cubes and record it on squared paper. Practical activity in small groups.	38
	100-square jigsaws	To recognize the number patterns that exist within a 100-square.	U&A 4a recognise simple patterns N 2a recognise sequences N 2b read and order numbers N 3b explore patterns in addition *Patterns and sequences, level B*	Count on or back in steps of 1, 10 or 100 (Y1/2 p2–5).	Pupils must reassemble a 100-square which has been cut up into several pieces. Practical activity in pairs.	40
	Number necklaces	To generate number sequences using the constant function of a calculator. To recognize and continue number sequences.	U&A 4a recognise simple patterns N 3b explore and record patterns in addition and subtraction, and then patterns of multiples *As above, level B*	Count on or back in steps of any size (Y1/2 p6–7).	The constant function on a calculator is used to generate number sequences which must be continued without the calculator. Calculator activity in pairs using a worksheet.	41

Dotty numbers, page 20

	ACTIVITY TITLE	LEARNING OBJECTIVE	POS/AO	NNS	CONTENT	PAGE
	Shading patterns	To identify and continue visual and numerical patterns in a 100-square. To practise mental counting-on skills.	U&A 4a recognise simple patterns and make related predictions N 3b explore and record patterns in addition and subtraction, and then patterns of multiples, using them to make predictions *As above, level B*	Count on or back in steps of any size (Y1/2 p6–7).	Pupils shade number sequences on the first five rows of a 100-square and pass it on to a partner to complete. Photocopiable sheet-based activity in pairs.	43

Number grids, page 40

ACTIVITY TITLE	LEARNING OBJECTIVE	POS/AO	NNS	CONTENT	PAGE
Stars and shapes	To mentally produce number sequences based on multiples. To use number sequences to produce visual patterns. To recognize similarities and differences in visual patterns.	U&A 4a recognise simple patterns and relationships N 2a count in steps of different sizes N 3b explore and record patterns in addition and subtraction, and then patterns of multiples *Patterns and sequences, level C*	Count on or back in steps of any size (Y1/2 p6–7). Recognise simple patterns or relationships (Y1/2 p62–63).	Number sequences are plotted on a special clock face to produce stars and other shapes. Individual drawing activity on a photocopiable sheet.	46
Dotty sequences	To identify numbers which belong to a particular set or sequence. To continue these number sequences.	N 2a count in steps of different sizes; recognise sequences N 3b explore and record patterns in addition and subtraction, and then patterns of multiples *As above, level B*	Recognise odd and even numbers (Y1/2 p4–5). Count on or back in steps of any size (Y1/2 p6–7).	Dot-to-dot puzzles in which pupils join the dots which belong to a particular set or sequence. Individual photocopiable sheet-based activity.	48
Dotty numbers, page 20					
Multilink sequences	To recognize and continue a visual sequence produced using practical apparatus. To identify numerical patterns associated with a visual sequence.	U&A 4a recognise simple patterns N 2a recognise sequences N 3a use repeating patterns to develop ideas of regularity and sequencing *As above, level A*	Recognise simple patterns or relationships (Y1/2 p62–63).	Pupils continue a sequence of multilink shapes which follow a clear visual pattern and also investigate the numerical patterns in the numbers of cubes. Practical activity working in small groups.	49
Hunt the domino	To identify a missing item from a set by using various sorting and ordering strategies.	N 3a use repeating patterns to develop ideas of regularity and sequencing N 5a sort and classify a set of objects *As above*	Solve mathematical problems or puzzles (Y1/2 p62–63). Solve a given problem by sorting or organising information (Y1/2 p90–91).	Pupils work out which domino is missing from the set and explain how they worked out the answer. Practical activity working in small groups.	52
Odd and even with dominoes	To identify odd and even numbers. To spot patterns and relationships when odd and even numbers are combined.	N 2a recognise sequences, including odd and even numbers N 5a sort and classify a set of objects *Patterns and sequences, level B*	Recognise odd and even numbers (Y1/2 p4–5).	Dominoes drawn on a photocopiable sheet are shaded according to whether they have an odd or an even number of spots. These are then sorted in various ways. Individual photocopiable sheet-based and practical activity.	54
Odd and even, page 50; Block graphs, page 86					
Go and stand with…	To decide whether or not a number belongs to a particular set. To identify the position of a number in a particular sequence. To practise mental arithmetic skills.	U&A 4a recognise simple patterns and relationships N 2a recognise sequences N 3b explore patterns in addition and subtraction, and then patterns of multiples. *As above*	Count on or back in steps of any size (Y1/2 p6–7). Recognise familiar multiples (Y1/2 p6–7).	Each pupil is identified by a number. Pupils get into lines and groups according to instructions from the teacher. Whole-class activity involving movement in a large open space.	56

ACTIVITY TITLE	LEARNING OBJECTIVE	POS/AO	NNS	CONTENT	PAGE
Sets and sequences	To identify numbers which belong to a particular set or sequence.	N 2a count in steps of different sizes; recognise sequences, including odd and even numbers N 3b explore patterns in addition and subtraction, and then patterns of multiples N 3c know addition facts *Patterns and sequences, level B*	Recognise odd and even numbers (Y1/2 p4–5). Count on or back in steps of any size (Y1/2 p6–7). Recognise familiar multiples (Y1/2 p6–7).	Pupils select those cards from a pack numbered 1-100 which belong to a specified sequence or set. Practical activity working in pairs or small groups.	58

CALCULATIONS AND PROBLEM SOLVING					
Domino additions	To develop knowledge of addition facts. To sort dominoes according to the sums of spots on each half.	N 3c know addition facts to 20 N 5a sort and classify a set of objects *Add and subtract, level B*	Understand the operation of addition and the related vocabulary (Y1/2 p24–25). Know by heart addition facts (Y1/2 p30–31). Solve a given problem by sorting or organising information (Y1/2 p90–91).	Pupils pick a domino, call out the addition which corresponds to the numbers on each half and then place it in the appropriate region of a sorting diagram according to the total. Practical activity working in groups.	60

Building up numbers, page 38; Addition and subtraction board games, page 42; The toy shop, page 56

Domino differences	To understand the notion of 'difference'. To develop knowledge of subtraction facts. To sort dominoes according to the differences between spots on each half.	N 3c know subtraction facts to 20 N 5a sort and classify a set of objects *As above*	Understand the operation of subtraction and the related vocabulary (Y1/2 p28–29). Know by heart subtraction facts (Y1/2 p30–31). Solve a problem by sorting or organising information (Y1/2 p90–91).	Pupils pick a domino, call out the subtraction which corresponds to the numbers on each half and then place it in the appropriate region of a sorting diagram according to the difference. Practical activity working in groups.	63

Subtraction patterns, page 39; Addition and subtraction board games, page 42; Change from 20p, page 57

Domino squares	To develop knowledge of addition facts. To apply this knowledge in a problem-solving situation.	N 3c know addition and subtraction facts to 20 N 4a use addition and subtraction to solve problems with whole numbers *As above*	Understand the operations of addition and subtraction and the related vocabulary (Y1/2 o24–29). Know by heart addition and subtraction facts (Y1/2 p30–31). Solve mathematical problems or puzzles (Y1/2 p62–63).	Two dominoes are placed together to form a square and pupils work out the row and column totals. Then a photocopiable sheet activity in which pupils find the dominoes which produce the given row and column totals. Practical problem-solving activity carried out individually.	65
Three in a row	To practise addition and subtraction facts in the context of a strategy game.	N 3c know addition and subtraction facts to 20 *As above, level B*	Know by heart addition and subtraction facts (Y1/2 p30–31).	Pupils pick two 0-9 number cards, use them to make an answer and then cover the appropriate number on a grid with a counter of their own colour. Aim is to get three counters in a row. Game for two players.	67

Addition and subtraction board games, page 42

ACTIVITY TITLE	LEARNING OBJECTIVE	POS/AO	NNS	CONTENT	PAGE
Addition with HTU cards	To consolidate understanding of place value. To develop and practise both mental and pencil and paper methods for addition.	N 2b develop an understanding that the position of a digit signifies its value N 3d develop a variety of methods for adding *Add and subtract, level C*	Use known number facts and place value to add a pair of numbers mentally (Y1/2 p36–39).	Pupils add pairs of two and three-digit numbers by first breaking each number up into its constituent parts using a special set of cards. Individual activity.	69
Arithmetic search	To develop knowledge of addition and subtraction facts.	N 3c know addition and subtraction facts to 20, and develop a range of mental methods *As above, level B*	Know by heart addition and subtraction facts (Y1/2 p30–31).	A grid contains many pieces of arithmetic. Pupils have to find complete and correct pieces of arithmetic and then make up a grid of their own for others to use. Individual photocopiable sheet-based activity.	72
Find...	To develop knowledge of addition facts involving numbers up to 20. To practise mental arithmetic skills.	N 3c know addition facts to 20, and develop a range of mental methods *As above*	Know by heart addition facts (Y1/2 p30–31). Understand that more than two numbers can be added together (Y1/2 p26–27).	Pupils must find pairs or groups of numbers on a grid which meet a particular specification. Individual photocopiable sheet-based activity.	73

Change from 20 pence, page 57; Change from £1, page 59

ACTIVITY TITLE	LEARNING OBJECTIVE	POS/AO	NNS	CONTENT	PAGE
Doubling bingo	To practise mental doubling strategies involving numbers up to 10.	N 3c learn multiplication facts relating to the 2s *Multiply and Divide, level B*	Derive doubles quickly (Y1/2 p52–53).	The teacher rolls a dice and the pupils can cross of either the number itself or its double. In later games pupils design their own bingo card with numbers of their own choice. Whole-class teacher-led game.	76
Doubling three-in-a-row	To practise mental doubling strategies involving single-digit numbers.	N 3c learn multiplication facts relating to the 2s *As above*	Derive doubles quickly (Y1/2 p52–53).	Pupils roll a dice, double the score and then cover the appropriate number on a grid with a counter of their own colour. Aim is to get three counters in a row. Dice game for two players.	78
Multiplication practice	To develop knowledge of multiplication facts involving 2s, 5s and 10s.	N 3c learn multiplication facts relating to the 2s, 5s and 10s *As above*	Know simple multiplication facts by heart (Y1/2 p52–53).	Pupils roll two dice, multiply the scores and cover the appropriate number on a grid with a counter of their own colour. Aim is to get three counters in a row. Dice game for two players.	80

Number quiz, page 44; Beginning multiplication, page 60; Multiplication as repeated addition, page 66

ACTIVITY TITLE	LEARNING OBJECTIVE	POS/AO	NNS	CONTENT	PAGE
Two coins in my pocket	To practise addition skills involving one and two-digit numbers in the context of money.	N 3c know addition facts to 20, and develop a range of mental methods for finding those they cannot recall N 4a use addition to solve problems with whole numbers, including situations involving money *Money, level B*	Solve simple word problems involving money (Y1/2 p68–69).	The teacher has two coins in her pocket. Pupils must investigate how much money she might have? Individual investigative activity.	82
A book of stamps	To practise addition skills involving one and two-digit numbers in the context of money.	N 3c know addition facts to 20, and develop a range of mental methods for finding those they cannot recall N 4a use addition to solve problems with whole numbers, including situations involving money *As above*	Solve simple word problems involving money (Y1/2 p68–69).	Pupils investigate the different amounts of postage which can be made using a particular book of stamps. Individual investigative activity.	83
The class shop, page 64; Class cafe, page 65					
Sorting with house cards	To identify similarities and differences in a set of objects. To sort a set of objects using a Carroll diagram.	N 5a sort and classify a set of objects using criteria related to their properties N 5b use a range of charts, diagrams, tables and graphs *Organise and display, level A*	Solve a given problem by sorting or organising information in simple ways (Y1/2 p90–91).	Practical sorting activity in pairs. Pupils sort a set of house cards using a Carroll diagram.	85
Multilink houses	To investigate the number of ways in which objects can be arranged. To classify objects using a sorting diagram.	N 5a sort and classify a set of objects using criteria related to their properties N 5b use a range of charts, diagrams, tables and graphs *As above*	Solve mathematical problems or puzzles (Y1/2 p62–63). Solve a given problem by sorting or organising information in simple ways (Y1/2 p90–91).	Pupils investigate the number of different multilink 'houses' that can be made when certain numbers of colours are available. Practical activity working individually.	88
Sorting with dominoes	To sort a set of dominoes according to the numbers of spots. To apply knowledge of odd and even numbers. To understand the relationship between odd and even numbers when they are added.	U&A 4a recognise simple patterns and relationships U&A 4c understand general statements N 2a recognise odd and even numbers N 5a sort and classify a set of objects using criteria related to their properties N 5b use a range of charts, diagrams, tables and graphs *Organise and display, level B*	Recognise odd and even numbers (Y1/2 p4–5). Solve a given problem by sorting or organising information in simple ways (Y1/2 p90–91).	Pupils sort a set of dominoes using a Carroll diagram. The sorting is based on the odd and even properties of the spots on each half and on the whole domino. Practical sorting activity in pairs.	90
Sorting using Carroll diagrams, page 81					

The number system and place value

Children cannot calculate effectively unless they have a sound understanding of the number system and place value. As teachers it is important to avoid the danger of rushing on too quickly to introduce arithmetic before pupils have had an opportunity to develop confidence and a 'feel for number'. Time needs to be spent on counting, ordering and making the links between physical objects, number symbols and the associated language. It is perfectly feasible for pupils to work with numbers up to 100, supported by visual aids such as number lines and 100-squares, without ever doing any 'sums'.

The activities in this section focus on several aspects: the reading, writing and ordering of numbers; the development of language associated with number; and place value. There are also two activities which introduce children to the concept of halves. Some of the activities make use of an electronic calculator but not as a substitute for mental arithmetic skills. Instead the calculator is used as a stimulus to promote the use of mathematical language and to consider the ordering and sequencing of numbers. Children will encounter digits presented in electronic displays almost every day and so this important aspect of number recognition is considered in some of the activities.

GIANT CALCULATOR

To develop language associated with position such as 'next to', 'between', 'above', 'below'. To recognize numbers and mathematical symbols.
†† *Whole-class activity.*
🕐 *Introduction 5–10 minutes; main activity 5–10 minutes; plenary 5–10 minutes; total 15–30 minutes.*

Previous skills/knowledge needed
This activity is suitable for very young children although it would be helpful if they are familiar with the number symbols 0–9 and have begun to use language associated with position.

Key background information
Children's later mathematical development is dependent on their ability to recognize numbers and symbols, to match objects, and to use mathematical language. This activity provides an opportunity for pupils to develop these important skills by looking at how numbers and other symbols are arranged on a calculator.

Preparation
Make a poster-size drawing of the type of calculator used in your school but do not include the calculator keys. The key-pad area of the poster should be left completely blank or you could draw just the outlines of the individual keys. Each number or symbol should be drawn on a separate piece of card to represent a calculator key. If your calculator uses different colours for different keys then you will need to use appropriately coloured card. At the start of the lesson fix the poster to the wall or an easel with all of the keys stuck in the appropriate places using Blu-Tack.

Resources
A poster-sized drawing of a calculator as described in 'Preparation', one calculator per pupil (or one between two pupils), Blu-Tack.

What to do
Introduction
Give out the calculators and ask the children to look carefully at what appears on the keys. Ask them various questions about the calculator keys, for example: *Can anyone tell me one of the numbers they can see on the keys? Do any of the keys not have numbers on them? Can you see any letters? What letter is it? Have you seen that symbol before? Do you know what it means? Are all the keys the same colour? What colour is the + key? Tell me what appears on one of the red keys.* There are many possible questions that can be asked and in all cases the aim is to encourage the children to describe what they can see using appropriate language. Use the poster as a visual aid when asking questions and following-up the pupils' responses.

Ask further questions involving language associated with position, for example: *Which key is next to the 7? Which key is above..., below..., between..., to the right of..., to the left of...?* Again, the poster can be used to give further explanations when necessary.

Main activity
Remove all of the keys from the calculator poster and ask individual children to come out one at a time and stick one of the keys back on to it. Allow children to bring their

display, perhaps using labelled arrows. Displays such as these would provide a constant reminder for the children and help them to become accustomed to the language.

Assessment opportunities
The children's responses throughout the activity will enable you to judge which pupils are developing an understanding of the language associated with position and whether they are able to recognize numbers and mathematical symbols.

Display ideas
The calculator poster could become a permanent feature in the classroom. At the start of each day remove all of the keys and ask one child (or two children) to replace them. Over a period of a few weeks every child should have a turn at sticking the keys on the calculator poster.

CALCULATOR LIGHT-STICKS

To be aware of the different ways that numbers can be drawn or displayed.

†† *Whole-class introduction followed by individual work and whole-class plenary.*

⊕ *Introduction 5–10 minutes; main activity 10–15 minutes; plenary 5–10 minutes; total 20–35 minutes.*

Previous skills/knowledge needed
Pupils should be able to write the numbers 0–10 and be familiar with working with numbers in this range.

Key background information
Even very young children will have come across displays in which the numbers do not appear exactly as we write them, for example on calculators, digital watches and a wide range of household electronic appliances. It is therefore important that pupils are able to recognize and read numbers displayed in electronic form. Most displays use an arrangement of seven 'light-sticks' to display each digit. By switching these sticks on or off the digits 0–9 can be displayed, for example the digit 8 is formed when all seven light-sticks are turned on.

Preparation
Make a large copy of the seven light-stick arrangement on a piece of paper to aid your explanations and discussions later. None of the light-sticks should be shaded in at this stage. Make copies of photocopiable page 93, one for each child plus extra copies for any children who move on to the extension activities.

Resources
Calculators (one for each child or one between two), photocopiable page 93, pencils. For the support activity –

---

calculator with them to refer to. You might want to start by giving the first pupil a fairly easy key, for example one of the corner keys. Use prompts and questions to help the pupils decide where their key should go, for example: *Is it to the left or to the right of the 2? How far to the right?* and so on. Ensure that you point in the appropriate direction when using the words 'right' and 'left' to help children understand their meaning.

Plenary
Remove the keys from the calculator poster and collect all of the calculators from the children. Ask some further questions about the calculator, for example: *Who can remember one of the keys in the top row?* (Point at the poster.) *Can you remember one of the keys in the right-hand column of the calculator?* (Again, point at the poster.) *Who can remember which key was in the bottom, left-hand corner?* Hold up one of the keys (choose an easy one, for example a corner key) and ask if anyone can remember where it goes. Ask a child to stick it on the poster. Do this with all of the keys, taking every opportunity to use positional language.

Suggestion(s) for extension
Throughout the activity match your questions to the abilities of the children. In this way you should be able to challenge the more able pupils in the class.

Suggestion(s) for support
Those children who are not confident in the use of positional language would benefit from access to a wall display showing key words and examples that illustrate their meanings. In particular many children have difficulties with 'right' and 'left' and so this could form the basis of a

calculators with large displays, enlarged copies of photocopiable page 93 (optional), strips of black card.

What to do

Introduction

Start by asking a child to come out and write the number 4 on the board. Then ask if anyone has seen the number 4 shown in a different way. Ask any children who say yes to come out and draw it. Possible ways of writing the number 4 are:

4   4   4

You may also like to discuss the fact that the number 3 is often written in two different ways. If the children have not mentioned electronic displays by this stage then provide prompts and ask further questions to get them thinking about this method. Ask the pupils to tell you where they have seen numbers displayed electronically. A calculator is a good example of this and can be demonstrated easily to the children.

3   3

Give out the calculators and tell the children to press a few keys so that a number appears in the display. Ask various questions about the display, for example: *Does the calculator display the numbers the same way as we write them? What is different about the way the calculator does it?* Tell the children to look closely at the display, perhaps tilting it slightly so that the light reflects off the screen in a particular way. Ask them if they can see how the calculator actually displays the numbers. Discuss the way the calculator does this, using terminology such as 'light-sticks' or 'light-bars'. Use the light-stick arrangement you prepared earlier as a visual aid. Choose a single-digit number and ask one of the children to come out and shade in the appropriate light-sticks on to your large copy.

Main activity

Give each child a copy of photocopiable page 93. Tell the children to look carefully at how the calculator displays the digits 0–9 and to record this on their photocopiable sheet by shading in the appropriate light-sticks. When they have done this they can use the remaining spaces on the

sheet to record any other interesting numbers, for example their house number, their telephone number, today's date, and so on.

Plenary

Finish off the session by discussing important points that have arisen during the activity, for example many children often record the digit 7 incorrectly (they omit the vertical stick on the left) so this could be discussed and demonstrated. You could also ask further questions such as: *Which digit uses the most light-sticks? Which digit uses the fewest? When the calculator displays a 1, does it use the two light-sticks at the left or the two at the right?* (You might also want to discuss issues related to the extension activities described below.)

Suggestion(s) for extension

Those children who complete the initial activity could investigate which letters of the alphabet can be formed by shading in light-sticks. These could be recorded on a separate copy of photocopiable page 93. The children could also find numbers in the display which look like words, for example when the number 77345 is entered and the calculator is turned upside down it looks like the word 'shell'. Ask children to explain what they have found to the rest of the class during the plenary.

Suggestion(s) for support

Some children might benefit from using a calculator with a large display and an enlarged copy of photocopiable page 93. Children with physical disabilities who are unable to colour-in effectively could use strips of black card to represent the light-sticks and move these about to make the various digits.

Assessment opportunities

Check during the main activity that pupils are able to read the digits in the calculator display by simply pointing to a digit and asking them what it is. The opportunities offered by this activity are related more to generic skills (for example, observational skills) and IT (see below) than to mathematics.

Opportunities for IT

The introductory discussion of electronic digital displays will contribute to pupils' knowledge and experience of ICT in the outside world which is an important part of the Key Stage 1 Programme of Study for Information Technology.

Display ideas

Numbers, letters and words formed by shading in light-sticks could be used to produce an interesting display.

Reference to photocopiable sheet

Photocopiable page 93 allows children to record numbers by shading in the appropriate light-sticks. It can be enlarged or reduced if you feel this makes it more appropriate for individual pupils.

SIX LIGHT-STICKS

To recognize and record numbers as they appear in an electronic display. To order one, two and three digit numbers.

†† *Whole-class introduction followed by individual work and whole-class plenary.*

⏱ *Introduction 5–10 minutes; main activity 15–20 minutes; plenary 10–15 minutes; total 30–45 minutes.*

Previous skills/knowledge needed

Children will need to be familiar with numbers beyond 100 (the largest number most children will encounter in this activity is 111) and with the way digits are displayed on a calculator. The previous activity 'Calculator light-sticks' introduces children to the way digits are displayed.

Key background information

Much early number work focuses on the ordering of numbers. This activity provides a valuable opportunity to practise such skills in an unusual context. Before ordering the set of numbers children must first find them, using criteria based on the way an electronic calculator displays digits.

Preparation

Children could record their answers using photocopiable page 93. If so you will need to make sufficient copies. However, the photocopiable sheet is not essential; children could record their work on plain or lined paper instead, particularly if they have already done the earlier activity 'Calculator light-sticks'.

Resources

Calculators (one for each child or one between two) photocopiable page 93 (optional), plain or lined paper, pencils, board/flip chart. For the support activity – a number line or 100-square.

What to do

Introduction

If the children have not carried out the earlier activity 'Calculator light-sticks' then the introduction needs to focus on the issues covered in that activity.

If the previous activity has already been covered then recap some of the important points by asking questions such as: *Who can remember how many light-sticks are used to display the digit 7? Can you think of a digit which is made from exactly five light-sticks? How many light-sticks are used to display the number 10?*

Main activity

Hand out the calculators and explain to the children that they must use them to find as many numbers as they can which use exactly six light-sticks. Give each child either a copy of photocopiable page 93 or some plain or lined paper on which to record their answers.

It is likely that many pupils will not realize that they are looking for numbers which use exactly six light sticks rather than simply digits. Point this out to individuals or to the whole class by giving hints or asking particular types of questions.

Some pupils might find a two-digit number (for example, 14) but not realize that the reverse (41) uses the same digits and therefore the same number of light-sticks. Provide prompts or ask questions, for example: *Can you think of another number which uses a 1 and a 4?*

When the children have found all of the numbers (these are 0, 6, 9, 14, 17, 41, 71 and 111) ask them to list them in order of size starting with the smallest.

Plenary

Ask pupils to come out one at a time and to record the answers on the board in order of size. Alternatively, children can come out and write one of the numbers onto a large piece of paper. When you have all eight numbers these can be arranged in order and pinned to the wall. Ask place value related questions such as: *How can we tell that 41 is bigger than 14? Which digit do we need to look at?*

You may also like to ask questions related to the 'Suggestion(s) for extension' which some pupils are likely to do (see below), for example: *What is the biggest number that uses exactly eight light-sticks?*

Suggestion(s) for extension

Ask children who complete the initial activity to try to find numbers that use exactly seven or eight light-sticks and to arrange them in order of size.

Suggestion(s) for support

If the children have carried out the previous activity 'Calculator light-sticks' they may benefit from having access to the sheet they completed then. They may also find it helpful to have a fresh copy of photocopiable page 93 on which to record their work. If you feel that the open-ended nature of the activity is not suited to some pupils, ask closed questions such as: *Which digits use exactly two light-sticks, three light sticks, four light-sticks…?* and so on. During the ordering part of the activity some children may benefit from having access to a number line or a 100-square.

Assessment opportunities

Observe children as they look for the numbers. For example, those who find 17 and then immediately realize that 71 is another possibility are demonstrating a sound understanding of place value. Check also children's lists of ordered numbers. This will give you an indication of their understanding of the size and order of numbers.

Display ideas

The numbers can be drawn calculator-style and displayed on the wall under various headings such as 'These numbers use exactly six light-sticks', 'These numbers use exactly eight light-sticks' and so on.

CALCULATOR FISHING

To recognize numbers when they are written in the style of an electronic display. To match the score on a dice shown as dots with the corresponding number in written form.

†† *Whole-class introduction followed by a game played in small groups. Alternatively this could be just one of several activities being carried out by different groups in the classroom.*

🕐 *Introduction 5–10 minutes; main activity 15–20 minutes; plenary 5–10 minutes; total 25–35 minutes.*

Previous skills/knowledge needed

Children will need to have done some early work on counting and be familiar with numbers up to 10.

Key background information

Children encounter numbers represented in various ways: as spots on a dice, as a numeral written in the usual way and in electronic form in the display of a calculator. This activity gives children an opportunity to make connections between these different representations by playing a game in small groups. It also encourages them to develop important social skills such as co-operating with one another and taking turns within a group.

Preparation

This will depend on how the game is to be played (see below). If you use the 'colouring-in' approach then ensure that there is a copy of photocopiable page 94 for each player plus additional copies if they play more than one game. If you use the 'cover with counters' approach then the initial preparation time is high but the resources produced can be used repeatedly. For this approach make copies of photocopiable page 94, colour them to make them look attractive (you could possibly get children to do this), trim each sheet to just less than A4 size, stick onto A4 card and then cover with clear plastic (or use a laminating machine). Produce enough of these so that each player has a copy.

Resources

One dice and one calculator per group, photocopiable page 94, pencils, colouring materials/supply of counters, board/flip chart. For the support activity – large dice and calculators.

What to do

Introduction

Rather than simply explaining how to play the game you may like to start by asking questions about the numbers that appear on a dice and on the keys of a calculator. Such questions could include: *What is the biggest score you can get on a dice? What is the smallest? What numbers can you see on the keys of this calculator? What is the biggest number? If I press the 4 key what will we see in the display? How does the calculator show the number 4 in the display?* and so on.

Main activity

Organize the children into small groups and give each group one dice and one calculator. Hand each player a copy of photocopiable page 94. Explain that, in turns, each child must roll the dice and work out what the score is. He or she should then find that number on the calculator key-pad, press the key, look in the display and then find a fish on his or her sheet which corresponds to that particular number. The child should then colour in the fish. Alternatively, the fish could be covered with a counter. Play then passes to the next pupil. The winner is the first pupil to colour in or cover all of his or her fish.

Plenary

Use the plenary to consolidate the children's knowledge of the calculator display. Say to them: *Who would like to come out and draw the number 1 as it appears in the calculator display?* Allow children to refer to a calculator when drawing the number on the board or flip chart. Repeat this with the other numbers that have been considered during the main activity.

Suggestion(s) for extension

More able pupils could use a ten-sided dice numbered 0–9, a twelve-sided dice numbered 1–12 or a twenty-sided dice numbered 1–20. An alternative is to use two six-sided dice and add the scores. In all of these cases you will need to adapt the numbers on the photocopiable sheet to reflect the range of scores possible on the dice being used.

Suggestion(s) for support

Some pupils might benefit from using a large dice and a calculator with a large display. Another possibility is for two pupils to share one copy of the photocopiable sheet, thus giving support to each other while playing the game.

Assessment opportunities

The speed at which pupils are able to work through the steps from rolling the dice to shading in a fish will indicate how well their recognition and matching skills are developing, particularly in the case of less able pupils.

Reference to photocopiable sheet

Photocopiable page 94 shows some fish numbered 1–6. The children are required to match numbers on a dice and calculator to numbers on the sheet.

Calculator fishing

FAST-FINGERS

To read, write and order one and two-digit numbers generated by a calculator. To develop and use correctly mathematical language associated with the size of numbers such as 'bigger than', 'smaller than', 'more than', 'less than', 'between'.

†† *Whole-class introduction followed by work in groups and a whole-class plenary.*

🕑 *Introduction 10–15 minutes; main activity 15–20 minutes; plenary 5–10 minutes; total 30–45 minutes.*

Previous skills/knowledge needed

Children should be familiar with numbers beyond 20 and have some experience of using a calculator.

Key background information

Many early number activities focus on the important skill of being able to order a set of numbers. This activity provides a context for pupils to develop these skills using numbers generated by a calculator. The activity also introduces a very powerful facility available on a calculator, that is, the constant function. Calculators can do much more than carry out complex calculations and check answers; they can be used even with very young pupils to demonstrate counting-on in 1s, 2s and so on, and to develop an understanding of size and order in the number system.

Preparation

Ensure that there are enough calculators, one per pupil. Cut up sheets of scrap paper into smaller pieces, large enough for the children to write a number on. Investigate how the constant function operates on the calculators you are using. In most cases you need to press:

But on some older calculators it is:

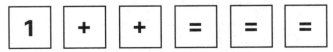

Resources

Calculators, small scraps of paper, writing materials, board/flip chart.

What to do

Introduction

Demonstrate the constant function to the children by talking them through the key presses described opposite. They should be able to make the calculator count on in 1s. Ask one of the pupils to describe what is happening to the numbers in the display.

You might want to use this as an opportunity to talk about large numbers. You could ask questions such as: *If we kept pressing the equals key for a long time what number do you think we could get to?* As children make suggestions ask them if they know how to write the number down. Write it on the board for everyone to see. Follow this up by asking if anyone knows an even bigger number. Again write it on the board. This could eventually lead on to a consideration of what the biggest possible number is and the fact that no matter how big a number is, you can always add 1 to get an even bigger number.

The next stage is to play 'Fast-fingers'. Tell the children to clear the calculator display. They should press 1 + = (or 1 + + =) and then fold their arms. When you say 'go' they must press the equals key as many times as they can until you say 'stop'. Then they must fold their arms again. Try this but do not give the children too much time or they will generate very large numbers. Aim for about five seconds although you can alter this depending on the sorts of numbers you want the children to work with. After you have said 'stop', ask various questions about the numbers the children have in their displays, for example: *Who has got a number bigger than 30? … less than 15? … between 20 and 25? … more than 35 but less than 40?* and so on. As children put their hands up, ask one of them what their number is just to make sure they are right. Pick up on any wrong answers by asking further questions.

Main activity

Organize the children into small groups to play 'Fast-fingers'. Hand out the small scraps of paper and explain that one child will act as timer while the others play the game. The timer says 'go', waits about five seconds and then says 'stop' (a good way for the child to time this is for him or her to say quietly 'one elephant, two elephants, …., five elephants'). Each child must then write down their number on a scrap of paper. Then they take it in turns to lay their number in a line across the table in order of size. Stress to the children that the object of the game is not to get the biggest number but for them to place their number in the correct position on the table. When all the numbers have been placed on the table the pupils can count on together to check that they are in the correct order. Children can take it in turns to be the timer.

Plenary

Use this time for further discussions about big numbers by asking questions such as: *What was the biggest number you had to write down? Can you remember what it looked like? Say the number for me. Did anyone get a number bigger than this?* and so on. Write the numbers on the board to assist the discussion.

You might also want to consider using the calculator to count on in 2s or 3s. Start by saying: *Suppose I pressed 2 + = = = (or 2 + + = = =). What do you think we would see in the display?* Discuss the children's responses and perhaps let them try it for themselves. This could be developed further another time (see the activity 'Number necklaces' on page 41).

Suggestion(s) for extension

Children who are capable of dealing with larger numbers

SQUEEZE

To develop and correctly use mathematical language associated with the size of numbers, for example, 'bigger than', 'smaller than', 'more than', 'less than', 'between'. To identify a number which lies between two given numbers.

†† *Whole-class introduction followed by individual work and whole-class plenary.*

⏱ *Introduction 5–10 minutes; main activity 15–20 minutes; plenary 5–10 minutes; total 25–40 minutes.*

Previous skills/knowledge needed

This activity is suitable for children who have had some experience of the size and order of numbers up to 10 and the associated language.

Key background information

Children's early experience of number involves counting and ordering numbers up to 10 and developing language such as 'bigger', 'smaller' and 'between'. They also need to be able to recognize and write the number symbols. A large number line or a row of numbers in order across the classroom wall is a valuable visual aid in developing this knowledge and understanding. This activity focuses on these important early aspects of number.

Preparation

Make sufficient copies of photocopiable page 95, one for each child. Obtain some assorted dice, not just six-sided ones. Ideally you should have enough for one for each child but children can share if you do not have enough.

Resources

Assorted dice, photocopiable page 95, pencils, number line. For the extension activity – various polyhedral dice and/or cards numbered from 1–100.

What to do

Introduction

Start by asking questions about the order and size of numbers up to 10, for example: *Who can tell me a number smaller than 5? … bigger than 8? … between 6 and 10?* and so on. Use a large number line or a row of numbers in order across the classroom wall as a visual aid to help the children.

Main activity

Give each child a dice and a copy of photocopiable page 95. Explain that they must roll the dice and write the score in the left-hand box. They must then roll the dice again and enter this score in the right-hand box. In the middle box they should then write a number that is between the two dice scores. Remind children that they can use the number line or row of numbers across the wall if they

could have longer than five seconds when playing 'Fast-fingers' in groups. (This assumes that the pupils have been grouped according to ability.)

Suggestion(s) for support

Spend time with the least able group during the main activity. Tell them to press the equals key just once and then ask: *What comes next?* Tell them to press the equals key once more to see if they were right and again ask: *What comes next?* See how far the pupils can go. Follow this by playing 'Fast-fingers', perhaps allowing them only two or three seconds so that the numbers reached are not so big.

Assessment opportunities

When asking questions during the introduction such as: *Who has got a number between 10 and 20?* ask the less able pupils who put their hands up to tell you their number. This will enable you to check whether they understand the mathematical language and the order and size of numbers. Also, during the main activity, you should learn a great deal about the pupils in the least able group by listening to their responses to your *What comes next?* questions and by observing them placing their number in order on the table.

Opportunities for IT

Pupils need to be able to access the facilities of an electronic calculator such as the constant function. This activity will give them practice in this area.

need help. Explain that if they do not think there is a number between the two dice scores then they should put a cross in the middle box.

Children can work in pairs, sharing a dice, rolling it once each and then filling in their own copy of photocopiable page 95.

Plenary

Discuss the occasions when it was not possible to write a number in the middle box. Ask questions such as: *Who had to draw a cross in the middle box? Why did you have to draw a cross? What were the dice scores? Is there a number which is between 3 and 4?* Using a number line as a visual aid, this could lead on to a discussion of halves. Many children, even at an early age, have some understanding of halves and so it is likely that there will be pupils in the class who can contribute to this discussion.

If appropriate explore the idea of a number being exactly half-way between two other numbers, depending on how many children have covered this during the main activity.

Suggestion(s) for extension

Pupils could use various polyhedral dice, for example a ten-sided dice numbered 0–9, a twelve-sided dice numbered 1–12 or a twenty-sided dice numbered 1–20. More able pupils could pick two cards from a pack numbered from, say, 1–100. Also, rather than simply writing down a number that lies between the other two they could write down the number exactly half-way between.

Suggestion(s) for support

Less able children could use a six-sided dice. Ensure that they have access to a number line either displayed on the wall or written on a strip of card for personal use.

Assessment opportunities

Make a mental note of the children's responses during the introduction and plenary, particularly the incorrect responses. Some children may still be having problems with language such as 'bigger than', 'smaller than'. The children's written work will give a valuable insight into their understanding of order and size.

Reference to photocopiable sheet

Photocopiable page 95 provides a format on which the children can record their dice throws and intermediate numbers.

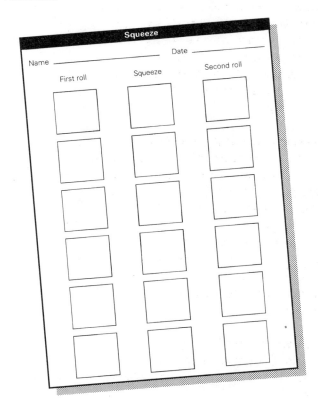

BOXES

To arrange numbers in order of size. To estimate where a number should come within a particular range.

†† *Whole-class introduction followed by work in pairs and a whole-class plenary.*

🕐 *Introduction 10–15 minutes; main activity 25–30 minutes; plenary 10–15 minutes; total 45–60 minutes.*

Previous skills/knowledge needed

Children should be familiar with numbers up to 100 although it is possible to adapt the main activity so that they are working with numbers only up to 10 or 20.

Key background information

Children are provided with many opportunities to order sets of numbers but they tend not to be given opportunities to estimate where a number comes within a given range. These estimating skills are necessary at Key Stage Two when doing work on measures, for example reading values from a scale, and so it is important that pupils are encouraged to make judgements about the relative position and size of numbers during Key Stage One.

Preparation

For the introduction and plenary you will need a length of rope or string to use as a washing line and a supply of

pegs. Write the numbers 1–20 on 20 pieces of paper, one number per piece. These will be pegged onto the washing line for the whole class to see and so should be reasonably large. Put the washing line up in the classroom making sure that it is long enough to hang ten pieces of paper on with some space between each one.

For the main activity make copies of photocopiable page 96, enlarged to A3 size. You will need one photocopiable sheet for each pair of pupils. You will also need a pack of cards for each pair. The number of cards in each pack and the actual numbers on them can be varied according to the ability of the pupils. Possible packs which could be made are:

▲ all of the numbers 1–50;

▲ all of the numbers 51–100;

▲ 50 assorted numbers in the range 1–100.

(The cards will need to be the same size as the boxes on the enlarged copies of photocopiable page 96.)

Resources

Washing line, pegs, sheets of paper numbered 1–20, enlarged copies of photocopiable page 96, various packs of number cards.

What to do

Introduction

Use only the sheets of paper numbered 1–10 for the introduction. Show the children the pieces of paper and tell them that these are numbered 1–10. Hold up one of the pieces as an example. Explain that you want the ten numbers to hang on the washing line in order with the smallest number on the left. Tell them that once a number has been pegged on the line it must not be moved to make room for another number, so they will have to think very carefully about where it should go. Select a child to come out, pick one of the numbers without looking, and then to hang the number in the appropriate place. When the number has been placed, ask the child to explain why that particular position was chosen. Ask the rest of the class if they agree with the chosen position, particularly if it is incorrect. If appropriate, ask the child if he or she wants to reposition the number. Repeat this, using a different child each time, until all ten numbers have been pegged on the line.

If you feel it is necessary you could take down the numbers and repeat the activity using the numbers 1–15. You will have to extend the length of the washing line to accommodate 15 pieces of paper.

Main activity

Organize the children into pairs. (If there is an odd number of pupils in the class then one of the pairs can become a group of three.) Give each pair an enlarged copy of photocopiable page 96 and one pack of cards. (If there is a group of three then one of them can fold the sheet in

half vertically and use only one set of boxes.) Shuffle the cards and place them face down. Tell the children to take it in turns to pick a card and then judge which is the best box in which to put the card. Once a card has been placed in a box it cannot be moved later. The aim is to fill all ten boxes with numbers in order with the smallest number at the bottom. The numbers in the boxes do not have to be consecutive; they just have to be in order of size. If a pupil picks a card and is unable to place it in a box then it should be placed on a 'reject' pile. Each player should have his or her own 'reject' pile because these will need to be counted at the end. The game stops when someone has filled all ten boxes or when the cards run out. In the latter case the winner is the pupil who has filled the most boxes.

Various point-scoring systems can be used, depending on the children's ability to carry out the necessary calculations. Here is one possibility:

1. If you fill ten boxes score 25 points.
2. All other players score 2 points for every box filled.
3. Everyone (including the winner) deducts 1 point for each 'reject'.
4. If the cards run out then apply only 2 and 3 above.

Try to make up a scoring system of your own, or ask the children to make one up and then discuss it with them after they have been playing for a while.

When the children have played a couple of times with a particular pack of cards give them a different pack to use.

Plenary

Repeat the washing-line activity, this time using the numbers 5–20 (or any other range of numbers). It is important to use ranges that do not always start at 1 so that the children have to make the necessary adjustments to their judgements. You could also pick ten

pieces of paper from a set numbered 1–20, making sure there is just enough room on the washing line for ten numbers (as is the case with the boxes game). As in the introduction, ask the pupils to justify their choice of position on the washing line.

Suggestion(s) for extension

The packs of cards can be matched to the ability of the pupils and so the activity can challenge even the most able children. For example, they could use a pack containing 50 assorted numbers in the range 125–210 or any other range of your choice.

Suggestion(s) for support

Less able children could use a pack with fewer cards containing lower numbers, for example a pack numbered 1–20. You may also like to adapt the photocopiable sheet so that they use only five boxes instead of ten.

Children could also pick from their own pack of cards numbered 1–10, so that they have ten boxes to be filled with the numbers 1–10.

Assessment opportunities

Children's responses during the introduction and plenary will provide valuable information about their understanding of order and size. Be aware of children who place or suggest placing a number in a position that is clearly incorrect. Ask them to justify their choice. During the main activity, observe children carefully as they place cards in the boxes, particularly those pupils who showed lack of understanding during the introduction. Ask pupils to explain their choice, particularly if it is clearly not a good one.

Opportunities for IT

A similar theme is explored in the program *Box* produced by MicroSMILE. This is available for BBC, RM Nimbus PC-186, Archimedes and Windows-based computers. The program can be used by individuals or pairs of children or alternatively you could use it with the whole class gathered around the computer on the carpet.

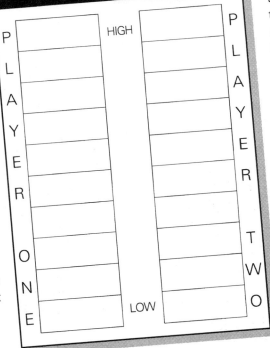

Reference to photocopiable sheet

Photocopiable page 96 provides ten blank boxes. The children must attempt to fill the boxes with their number cards, placing them in order of size.

GUESS THE NUMBER

To use and understand mathematical language associated with size and order.

†† *Whole-class introduction followed by work in pairs or small groups and a whole-class plenary.*

🕐 *Introduction 10–15 minutes; main activity 15–20 minutes; plenary 5–10 minutes; total 30–45 minutes.*

Previous skills/knowledge needed

Children need to be familiar with numbers up to at least 20 and have some experience of language associated with size and order.

Key background information

During Key Stage One, pupils must develop a thorough understanding of the size and order of numbers and the language that accompanies it since this underpins all of the number work that follows. This activity provides an opportunity to reinforce and develop this knowledge and understanding. It also requires pupils to work logically, devising their own questions to identify a mystery number by a process of elimination.

Preparation

Each pair or small group of pupils will need a set of 1–20 number cards. The sets of cards can be varied according to the ability of the pupils as described in the 'Suggestion(s) for extension and support' sections.

Resources

A set of 1–20 number cards for each pair or small group of children, a number line (optional).

What to do

Introduction

Tell the children that you have thought of a number and they must try to work out what it is by asking questions to which you will answer either 'yes' or 'no'. Think of a number, appropriate for the age and ability of the pupils and then invite them to ask questions. They may start by asking questions such as: *Is it 7? Is it 4?* Point out that these are not very good questions and discuss the reasons why. Suggest other types of question they could ask based on language such as 'odd', 'even', 'more than', 'less than' and so on. Continue to play the game and see how many questions are required to guess the number. A large number-line could be used as a visual aid to show children where your number could lie. Play this whole-class game as many times as you feel is necessary. A variation is to allow one of the pupils to think of the number and respond 'yes' or 'no' to the questions.

Main activity

Arrange the children into pairs or small groups and tell them they will be playing a similar game. Hand out the set of 1–20 number cards and tell them to lay them out on the table facing upwards. One child must mentally pick one of the cards without identifying it to the others. The other children must work out which card it is by asking questions that have a 'yes' or 'no' answer. After each question has been answered those numbers which have been eliminated can be removed from the table. Children must try to identify the number using the fewest number of questions.

Plenary

Ask the children to explain how they decided what sorts of questions to ask. Discuss examples of good and not so good questions. You may like to repeat the game played during the introduction, but this time choose a number which is not a whole number, for example 6½. When the children have asked a few questions and established that your number is more than 6 but less than 7 some may appear puzzled. However, this is a gentle way to start looking at non-integral numbers. Again, a large number line is a useful visual aid.

Suggestion(s) for extension

The sets of number cards can be adjusted according to the ability of the pupils, for example some children could use a set numbered 1–50. The most able pupils might prefer to use numbers up to and beyond 100 without using number cards.

PLACE VALUE WITH HTU CARDS

To understand that the position of a digit affects its value.

†† *Whole-class introduction followed by work in groups and a whole-class plenary.*

⏲ *Introduction 5–10 minutes; main activity 25–30 minutes; plenary 5–10 minutes; total 35–50 minutes.*

Previous skills/knowledge needed

Children need to be familiar with three-digit numbers although some pupils could work with only two-digit numbers.

Key background information

An understanding of place value is crucial if children are to develop good mental maths skills. This activity provides an opportunity to demonstrate to pupils that the position of a digit in a number affects its value.

Preparation

Each group of pupils will require a complete set of HTU cards. Photocopiable pages 97–100 need to be photocopied onto card and then cut up to make the sets of HTU Cards. (There will be 18 cards in a set if the pupils are to make two-digit numbers and 27 if they are to make three-digit numbers.) Also make copies of photocopiable page 101 so that there is one for each pupil. Photocopiable page 102 is provided for use in the support activity by less able pupils.

Suggestion(s) for support

The sets of cards can be adjusted according to the ability of the pupils and so the least able could use a set numbered 1–10. Such pupils would also benefit from your assistance or that of a parent helper, particularly when they are trying to think of appropriate questions to ask.

Assessment opportunities

Listen carefully to the children's questions both during the whole-class game and when they are working in pairs or small groups. This will give an indication of whether they understand the general principles being used to work out the number. Also listen to the variety of language being used. Pupils may use alternatives to 'more than' and 'less than'. These alternatives could be discussed during the plenary.

Opportunities for IT

A similar theme is explored in the program *Guess* produced by MicroSMILE. This is available for BBC, RM Nimbus PC-186, Archimedes and Windows-based computers.

Display ideas

The words and phrases associated with the order and size of number, for example 'more than', 'less than', 'bigger than', 'between', and so on, can be written on pieces of card and displayed on the wall. These could be displayed alongside the number cards to illustrate how the words can be used.

Resources

Photocopiable pages 97–102, writing materials, board/flip chart.

What to do

Introduction

Ask a child to give you an example of a two-digit number and then ask him or her to come out and write it on the board. While the child is doing this, make the same number with your set of HTU cards. If, for example, the pupil has written 74 on the board, ask the pupils what the 4 represents. Similarly, ask them what the 7 represents. Use the HTU cards to show that the 7 represents 70. Repeat this with another two-digit number. Next, move on to using a three-digit number. Ask the children what each of the digits represents and demonstrate this using the HTU cards.

The HTU cards can also be used in a slightly different way. Hold up three cards separately, a units card, a tens card and a hundreds card. Ask the children to suggest the three-digit number that can be made by combining these three cards.

Main activity

Organize the children into groups and hand out one set of HTU cards per group. Give each pupil a copy of photocopiable page 101. Tell them to place the cards on the table face down. One child picks a units card, a tens card and a hundreds card and places these together to form a three-digit number. (The triangle at the right-hand side of each card is there to help align the cards. The units card, the tens card and the hundreds card should be held so that the triangles are aligned and held in place between thumb and fingers.) The child should try to form the number without letting anyone else see the three separate cards. The child then holds up the three-digit number. Everyone else in the group must write down the number in the appropriate place on their photocopiable sheet and also fill in the rest of that line. When everyone has finished, the pupil who formed the number separates the three cards to reveal the constituent parts. The other children can check to see whether they were correct. This is then repeated, but with a different pupil picking the three cards each time.

When a group has completed the photocopiable sheet, ask them to list all of the three-digit numbers in order of size. (They can use the back of their photocopiable sheet.)

A variation on this activity is to work the other way round. A child picks a units card, a tens card and a hundreds card and holds these up for everyone to see. The other pupils write down the three numbers on the photocopiable sheet and also work out the resulting three-digit number.

Plenary

Focus discussion on the ordering of the three-digit numbers and the strategies used by the children. Ask questions such as: *How do you know that 327 is bigger than 184? Which digit did you look at?*

Suggestion(s) for extension

Once pupils are able to work both ways using the HTU cards they can move on to similar activities using four-digit numbers, for example writing the number 4825 as 4000 + 800 + 20 + 5. Many pupils will be able to do this without using the cards, although you could make a set of thousands cards if necessary.

Suggestion(s) for support

Less able children could use a restricted set of cards (using only those made from photocopiable pages 97 and 98) and so make only two-digit numbers. They will then need a copy of photocopiable page 102 on which to record their work.

Assessment opportunities

The completed photocopiable sheets will provide valuable assessment evidence and indicate which pupils require further practice of this sort.

Display ideas

The HTU cards can be displayed on the wall to illustrate how a number can be split into its constituent parts and also the reverse process. This would provide a constant reminder to the children and aid their understanding of place value.

Reference to photocopiable sheets

Photocopiable pages 97–100 provide a set of HTU cards which the children use to create different two and three-digit numbers. They use photocopiable pages 101 and 102 to record the numbers.

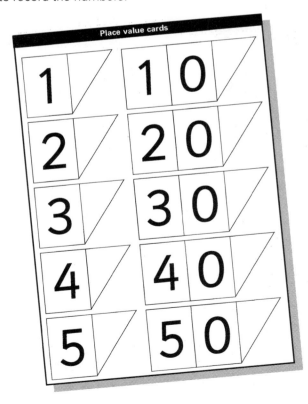

MAKING NUMBERS

To be able to make one, two and three-digit numbers from a list of digits provided. To order a set of one, two and three-digit numbers.

†† *Whole-class introduction followed by individual work and whole-class plenary.*

⏲ *Introduction 5–10 minutes; main activity 25–30 minutes; plenary 15–20 minutes; total 45–60 minutes.*

Previous skills/knowledge needed

Children will require a knowledge of one, two and three-digit numbers and some understanding of place value involving whole numbers.

Key background information

This open-ended activity gives children a valuable opportunity to develop their understanding of place value by asking them to make and then order various numbers. Other opportunities for this sort of work can be found in the activities 'Six light-sticks' on page 17, 'Place value with HTU cards' on page 27 and 'Place value dice games' on page 32.

Preparation

Ensure that each pupil has their own set of 0–9 number cards. Photocopiable page 103 can be used to produce these sets.

Resources

One set of 0–9 number cards per child (use photocopiable page 103 if necessary), pencils, paper.

What to do

Introduction

Ask the children to explain what is meant when we say 'two-digit number' or 'three-digit number'. Ask them to give examples of one, two and three-digit numbers. Build up a collection of one, two and three-digit numbers on the board. You might like to ask them which of these numbers is the biggest, the smallest, the smallest two-digit number, the biggest two-digit number and so on. Also, ask them how they know that the chosen number is the biggest or the smallest, encouraging them to think about and explain place value.

Main activity

Give each child a set of 0–9 number cards and some paper. Tell them that they must pick three cards from the set and then use the three digits to make as many different numbers as possible. Make it clear that they can make one, two and three-digit numbers. If they pick a zero they must put it back and pick another card instead (they could remove the zero before they start the activity).

Demonstrate an example to begin with. Pick three cards from a pack and ask the children to give an example of a two-digit and a three-digit number which can be made. Tell them to write down all the numbers they make with their three digits.

Set the children to work individually. While they are working, check their lists of numbers for errors, duplicates and omissions. It is likely that many pupils will have incomplete lists so you could prompt them with the necessary hints and clues to help them.

When pupils have produced a complete list (there should be three one-digit, six two-digit and six three-digit numbers) ask them to list the numbers in order of size.

Next ask the children to pick three new digits and again to list all of the possible numbers that can be made. This time though they should write them down in order of size from the outset. This will encourage pupils to think carefully about place value. Remind them not to use zero.

Plenary

Ask the children how many one, two and three-digit numbers it is possible to make with three digits. Tell them to explain to the rest of the class how they went about finding the numbers. Did they do it in a systematic way to avoid omissions?

Ask the children what would happen if they had used zero. For example, would it still be possible to make 15 different numbers with the digits 6, 0 and 2? (You can make only 11: three one-digit, four two-digit and four three-digit.) Ask pupils to give reasons for their answers. You could use a calculator to demonstrate what happens when you try to enter 062.

Ask the children what might happen if they picked a card, replaced it, picked another, replaced it and then picked another. For example, suppose they picked 7, 4 and 7. Would it still be possible to make 15 different numbers? (You can make only eight: two one-digit, three two-digit and three three-digit.) Ask pupils to give you reasons for their answers.

The use of zero and repeated digits could form the basis of a follow-up activity on a later occasion.

Suggestion(s) for extension

More able pupils could pick four digits (still not using zero) and write down all the possible numbers in order. You can make 64 numbers; four one-digit, 12 two-digit, 24 three-digit and 24 four-digit.

Suggestion(s) for support

Less able children could pick just two digits and make all the possible one and two-digit numbers.

Assessment opportunities

While the children are compiling their lists of numbers, observe the approaches they use. Do they list them randomly or are they more systematic? Ask them to explain how they are doing it. This will give an insight into their ability to think logically.

Those children who can list the numbers in order straightaway, without having already written them down, are demonstrating a sound understanding of place value.

Reference to photocopiable sheet

Photocopiable page 103 provides a set of 0–9 number cards that can be photocopied and cut out as a resource for the children. The cards can be laminated to make them more durable.

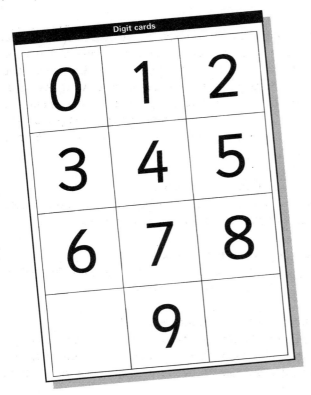

Digit cards

0 1 2
3 4 5
6 7 8
9

NUMBER FLIP-FLAPS

To generate numbers which fit certain criteria. To understand and correctly use mathematical language associated with the size and order of numbers.

†† *Whole-class introduction followed by individual work and a whole-class plenary.*

🕐 *Introduction 10–15 minutes; main activity 30–35 minutes; plenary 5–10 minutes; total 45–60 minutes.*

Previous skills/knowledge needed

Children should be familiar with numbers up to 100. They will also need to be able to use a pair of scissors and glue together pieces of card.

Key background information

It is important that children spend time developing an understanding of the number system before they move on to do arithmetic. This activity provides an opportunity for them to do this by focusing on the size and order of numbers up to 100 and the associated mathematical language. Pupils should be highly motivated by the creative and practical nature of this activity.

Preparation

Make copies of photocopiable sheet 104 onto card. Make copies of photocopiable page 105 onto paper. Pupils will need one copy of each sheet. Ensure that sufficient pairs of scissors are available as well as glue or sticky tape.

Resources

Photocopiable pages 104 (on card) and 105 (on paper), scissors, glue or sticky tape, pencils.

What to do

Introduction

Demonstrate to the children how to cut out the number flip-flap from the sheet of card. Pay particular attention to the cutting out of the inner square. Show them how to fold along each number square both ways to make the card pliable and how to stick the appropriate squares together using glue or sticky tape.

When you have made your flip-flap, show the children how it can be folded in many different ways to make two-digit numbers (the numbers must be read horizontally in the normal way, not vertically). Some of the digits have deliberately been drawn so that they can be read even when turned upside-down (0, 1, 6, 8 and 9.) Give the flip-flap to one of the pupils and ask him or her to make a particular number, for example a number less than 20, more than 50, between 30 and 40, and so on.

Main activity

Give each child a copy of photocopiable page 104 and instruct them to first cut out and assemble their number flip-flap. Next, give out the copies of photocopiable page 105 and tell them to use the flip-flap to complete the problems on the sheet.

Plenary

Focus discussion on some of the answers to the problems posed on the photocopiable sheet, for example how many different numbers less than 20 did the children find? You could also use this as an opportunity to reinforce other aspects of mathematical language by asking questions such as: *Did anyone find an even number less than 20? Did anyone find an odd number between 50 and 60?* and so on.

Suggestion(s) for extension

More able pupils could make three-digit numbers, record these and then arrange them in order of size.

Suggestion(s) for support

Devise questions and activities for the less able children that involve numbers only up to 20 or 50.

Assessment opportunities

The children's written answers on photocopiable page 105 will provide an indication of whether they understand the language associated with the size and order of numbers up to 100.

1. Cut out the number square.
2. Cut out the empty centre square.
3. Fold the number square in half.

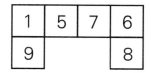

4. Stick the back of the 9 and 4 together and the back of the 8 and 3.
5. Score along the sides of the other numbers so that they can be bent and folded easily

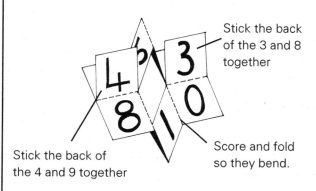

Stick the back of the 3 and 8 together

Stick the back of the 4 and 9 together

Score and fold so they bend.

Display ideas

'Number flip-flaps' can form the basis of an on-going class activity and display. Make a large 100-square and display it on the wall. Shade in any numbers that can be made with the flip-flap. Over a period of time the children can shade in any additional numbers they find. They could take their flip-flap home and try to find new numbers, perhaps with the aid of a parent. You could start every day by asking: *Has anyone found any new flip-flap numbers that we can shade in on the 100-square?*

Reference to photocopiable sheets

Photocopiable page 104 provides the format for a number 'flip-flap'. The children should be able to make more than forty numbers. Photocopiable page 105 poses a number of problems which the children have to work out using their number flip-flaps.

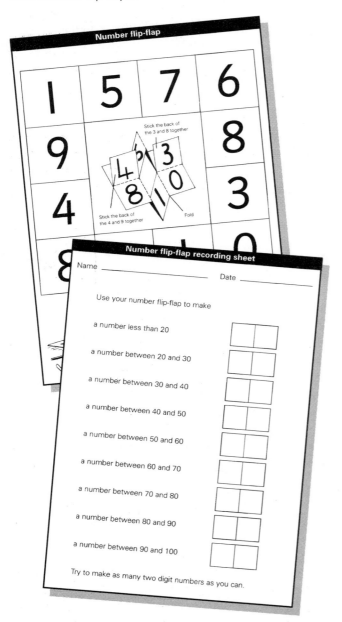

PLACE VALUE DICE GAMES

To understand that the position of a digit affects its value. To order a set of two-digit numbers.

†† *Whole-class introduction followed by work in pairs and a whole-class plenary.*

🕐 *Introduction 10–15 minutes; main activity 15–20 minutes; plenary 5–10 minutes; total 30–45 minutes.*

Previous skills/knowledge needed

Children should have some experience of working with numbers up to 100.

Key background information

In order to develop efficient mental maths skills children need to have a thorough understanding of place value. The game described in this activity is enjoyable and will motivate pupils, but more importantly it will help them to develop their understanding of place value.

Preparation

Make copies of photocopiable page 106 – one sheet for each pair of children. Also make some additional copies so that children who finish early can play extra games. Each pair will also need a ten-sided dice with faces numbered 0–9. An alternative to rolling the dice is to pick a card from a set numbered 0–9. Photocopiable page 103 can be used to produce these sets.

Resources

Photocopiable page 106, ten-sided dice (or sets of 0–9 number cards made using photocopiable page 103), pencils, board/flip chart, paper.

What to do

Introduction

Ask a child to roll a ten-sided dice (or pick a card from a set of 0–9 number cards) and tell you the score. Write it on the board. Repeat this to get a second digit. Ask questions such as: *Which two-digit numbers can be made from these? Which one is the bigger? How can you tell*

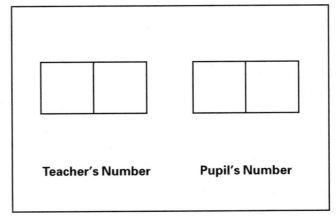

Teacher's Number　　　**Pupil's Number**

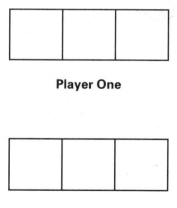

Player One

Player Two

which number is the bigger? and *Which digit do you use to help you decide?*

Next demonstrate to the children how to play the dice game. Draw an arrangement of boxes on the board like the ones on page 32.

You will be playing against one of the pupils. Each of you will roll the dice (or pick a card from a set of 0–9 number cards) twice. After each roll write the digit in one of your own boxes. After four rolls you will each have made a two-digit number. The winner is the person with the biggest number. Play the game a couple of times and talk through some of the decisions that have to be made, for example if your first roll is an 8 or a 9 where is the best place to put it?

Next introduce a new rule. Explain that now you can write the digit in one of your own boxes or in one of your opponent's boxes. Play the game a couple of times and again talk through some of the decisions that have to be made. Leave the results of the final game on the board – you can use them in the plenary.

Main activity
Organize the children into pairs and give each pair a copy of photocopiable page 106. Tell them to play the game using the same rules as the game you have just played (pupils can write their digit in their own or their opponent's box) recording their numbers on the sheet. Various scoring systems could be used. The simplest is for the winner to score one point. An alternative is for the winner to score

whatever their two-digit number is. Another alternative is for the winner to score the difference between the two two-digit numbers. The use of these scoring systems will obviously depend upon the children's ability to cope with the necessary arithmetic.

When the children have completed the sheet they can arrange all of their own two-digit numbers in order of size. Have some spare photocopiable sheets available so that early finishers can play additional games.

Plenary
Discuss the children's strategies when deciding in which box to put a digit. Some decisions are easy (for instance when you roll a 0, 1, 8 or 9) but what do you do if you roll a 5 or a 6?

Explain the third scoring system described above. Refer back to the last game you played during the introduction (the results should still be on the board) and ask pupils to work out how many points the winner would score using this system. Ask further questions such as: *How must the digits be arranged so that maximum points are scored?* and *What is the maximum number of points you can score in one game?*

Suggestion(s) for extension
More able pupils could roll the dice three times each and so generate three-digit numbers. They could draw their own boxes or you might like to produce a sheet for them to use which looks something like this.

These children could also use more complex scoring systems based on the numbers generated.

Suggestion(s) for support
Less able children should still find this activity accessible, although they might benefit from being able to see a large 100-square or a 0–100 number line displayed on the wall to help them appreciate the order and size of the numbers.

Assessment opportunities

Observe the children while they are playing the game and question them about their decisions. This should give an insight into their understanding of place value.

Reference to photocopiable sheet

Photocopiable page 106 provides boxes in which the children record their dice throws. It can also be adapted to accommodate three-digit numbers.

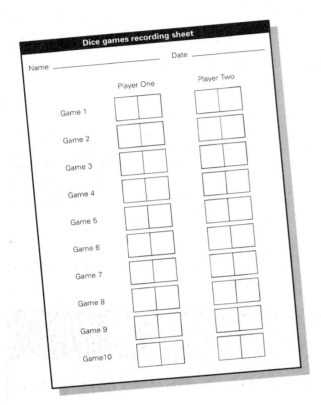

SHADE HALF

To understand what is meant by 'half'. To shade half of a square in several different ways.

†† *Whole-class introduction followed by individual work and whole-class plenary.*

🕐 *Introduction 5–10 minutes; main activity 20–25 minutes; plenary 5–10 minutes; total 30–45 minutes.*

Key background information

At Key Stage One, pupils need to be able to recognize and use simple fractions such as halves and quarters. This can be introduced and reinforced through many different practical activities such as the one described here.

Preparation

Cut out two or three squares from large sheets of paper to use during the introduction.

Resources

Two or three large squares (see 'Preparation'), pair of scissors, sheets of squared paper, rulers, pencils.

What to do

Introduction

Hold up one of the large square pieces of paper. Ask the children if they know what shape it is and discuss its important features. Then explain to them that you want to cut the square in half. Ask the pupils to explain how this could be done. Discuss the key mathematical point: the two pieces must be the same size. Use questions such as: *How do you know that this cut will produce two halves?*

Plenary
Use the plenary as a further opportunity to hold up, praise and discuss pupils' work.

Suggestion(s) for extension
This activity is differentiated by outcome and so the more able pupils will be those who find the most ambitious ways of shading half of the square.

Suggestion(s) for support
Prepare sheets of squared paper with 4 × 4 squares already drawn on them. Less able pupils would therefore not be delayed by having to draw the squares and instead be able to concentrate on the concept of a half. Also, some children might benefit from working in pairs.

Assessment opportunities
The children's completed pieces of work and their responses during the discussion periods will provide an insight into their understanding of the concept of a half. Also, question them while they are working on the main activity. Ask them to explain how they know that they have shaded in half of the square.

Display ideas
The visual nature of the work produced during this activity would make it ideal for display.

FRACTIONS WITH PATTERN BLOCKS

To understand what is meant by 'half'. To identify amounts that are more than or less than a half.

†† *Whole-class introduction followed by individual work and whole-class plenary.*

⏱ *Introduction 5–10 minutes; main activity 30–35 minutes; plenary 10–15 minutes; total 45–60 minutes.*

Previous skills/knowledge needed
Children should have some understanding of halves.

Key background information
Many early maths activities focus on the concept of a half but this tends not to be taken further to look at amounts that are more than or less than a half. In this activity pupils use Pattern blocks to fill shapes according to various criteria based on the idea of a half, more than a half and less than a half. Pattern blocks are ideal for this sort of shape-filling work because they can be physically manipulated to demonstrate a particular point. For example, if you want to convince a pupil that the star shape they have filled is half yellow and half green you can place the green pieces on top of the yellow piece to show that they take up the

How can you tell? What is special about the two pieces? and so on. You could explain it in terms of both pieces having the same amount of paper. Cut the paper as suggested by the pupils and then discuss whether or not you have got two halves. Repeat this with another square of paper, this time asking for a different way of cutting it in half.

Main activity
Give each pupil a sheet of squared paper, a ruler and a pencil. Explain that using the ruler, they must draw a 4 × 4 square on the squared paper. Explain and demonstrate this to them carefully. Then they must shade half of the square. Stress that half of the square must be shaded and half of the square must be left unshaded. Then they must draw another 4 × 4 square and shade half in a different way. Pupils should repeat this as many times as possible so that each 4 × 4 square shows a different way of shading half.

After they have been working for a while, stop and hold up some of the children's shadings. Discuss whether or not the pupil has shaded half of the square and how we can tell. Many pupils tend to stick to fairly routine ways of shading half so choose particularly interesting or unusual ones to discuss, for example one child may have produced a chequered pattern, another one may comprise of four vertical (or horizontal) stripes. These examples should prompt the rest of the class to look for further possible ways of shading half.

same space. Similarly, you can demonstrate that there is more or less of one colour than another.

Preparation

Draw several different shapes on the board or on large pieces of paper. Use shapes such as a square, rectangle, triangle, hexagon and circle. Shade in part of each shape so that at least one shape is exactly half-shaded, one shape less than half-shaded and at least one shape more than half-shaded. You will use these shapes during the introduction. Also make copies of photocopiable pages 107, 108 and 109 – one for each pupil for the main activity. (These may need to be enlarged or reduced by a small factor if you are not using standard size Pattern blocks. Ensure that your Pattern blocks will fit the outlines of the shapes on the sheets.)

Resources

Tubs of Pattern blocks (two tubs should be enough for a class of 30 pupils), photocopiable pages 107, 108 and 109, coloured pencils or crayons (blue, green, red and yellow).

What to do

Introduction

Show the class the shaded shapes you have prepared. Start by talking about the names and properties of each of the shapes. Then move on to ask questions about fractions, such as: *Which shape has exactly half shaded in? Which shape has less than half shaded in? Which shape has more than half shaded in?* If possible try to find examples around the classroom of objects that are half of one colour and half of another, or examples that are more than half of one

colour. Bring these to the children's attention and talk about them.

Main activity

Give each pupil a copy of photocopiable page 107 and tell them to follow the instructions. They must fill each shape with Pattern block pieces according to the instructions on the sheet and then shade the shape in the appropriate colours. Stress to the pupils that they must always use exactly two colours (two different types of Pattern block pieces) each time. Once they have completed photocopiable page 107 they can move on to pages 108 and 109.

Pupils will use only the yellow hexagon, the red trapezium, the blue rhombus and the green triangle in this activity and so will require pencils or crayons in those colours. The orange square and the brown rhombus are not used and so you might want to remove these from the tubs of Pattern blocks, although this is not essential.

Plenary

Use the plenary to go through the solutions to each problem. Ask the children to hold up their work and explain which pieces they used to fill the shape. There is often more than one way of doing it. For example you can fill the triangle labelled 'less than half blue' using just a single blue rhombus or using two of them, and in both cases the pieces can be arranged in several different positions. All of these things could be discussed with the pupils.

It is impossible to fill the triangle with half of one colour and half of another. You could discuss this with the pupils. One of them might be able to explain why it is impossible.

Suggestion(s) for extension

Able children might be able to explain why it is impossible to fill the triangle with 'half green'. Ask them to write this down in their own words. Also have a look at their other solutions. Every question can be answered in such a way that the shaded shape has a line of symmetry. If any of the children's solutions do not have a line of symmetry, ask them to find another solution which does.

If some pupils are familiar with quarters, ask them to try to fill the hexagon, the triangle and the star so that one-quarter is of one colour and three-quarters is of another. They could also try this with thirds.

Suggestion(s) for support

Some pupils may not be ready for the idea of more than or less than a half so they could focus on exact halves. You could provide various shapes drawn on a worksheet which can be filled with Pattern Blocks pieces so that half is of one colour and half is of another. These do not have to be regular shapes.

Assessment opportunities

The completed photocopiable sheets will provide an indication of whether children understand the concepts of half, more than half and less than half.

Opportunities for IT

Pupils can tackle similar problems using Logo. Write procedures to draw starting shapes such as squares, triangles, hexagons, stars, and so on. The children can type instructions to divide each shape according to your specifications and then shade the two parts using different colours.

Display ideas

The completed photocopiable sheets will be very colourful and eye-catching and so would make an excellent display.

Reference to photocopiable sheets

Photocopiable pages 107–109 show various shapes which the children have to fill according to the instructions on the sheet.

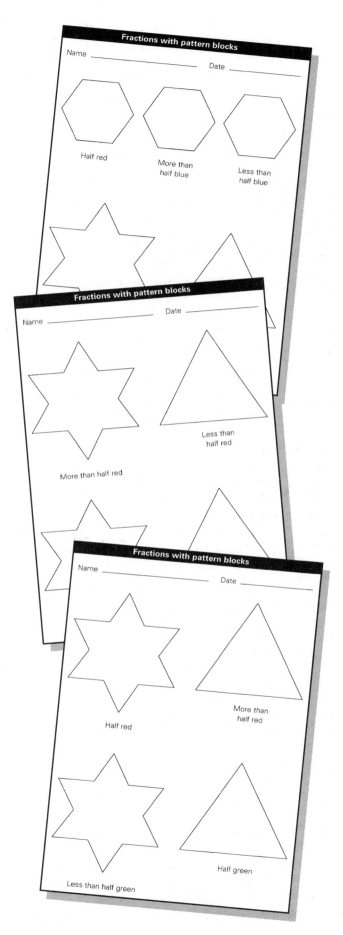

Number relationships

Pattern lies at the heart of much work in mathematics at all levels and so it is important that children are made aware of pattern at an early age. Initially these patterns are likely to be in purely visual terms but children will quickly be able to move on to consider the patterns and relationships that exist in our number system. Often visual and numerical patterns can be brought out in a single activity and children need to be aware of the co-existence of the two. They will need to be able to spot patterns, continue patterns and eventually make predictions based on these patterns.

The activities in this section focus mainly on the identification and continuation of both visual and numerical patterns, although there are opportunities for more able children to make predictions based on patterns (these are described in the 'Suggestion(s) for extension' section of particular activities). Many of the activities adopt a practical, 'hands-on' approach and explore pattern using a wide range of resources, such as multilink cubes and dominoes. Calculators are used to generate number sequences but never as a substitute for mental arithmetic skills.

REPEATING PATTERNS

To understand what is meant by the expression 'repeating pattern'. To recognize and continue a repeating pattern using practical apparatus. To draw a repeating pattern.

†† *Whole-class introduction followed by work in small groups and whole-class plenary.*

🕐 *Introduction 5–10 minutes; main activity 20–25 minutes; plenary 5–10 minutes; total 30–45 minutes.*

Key background information
Before children start to explore number patterns they need to be able to spot and continue purely visual patterns in a variety of contexts and using a wide range of practical apparatus. In this activity multilink cubes are used to explore repeating patterns based on colour and position.

Preparation
For the main activity each group will require a starting strip of multilink cubes that form a repeating pattern. These strips should comprise about six to eight cubes and the complexity of the pattern should reflect the ability of the pupils in the group. Prepare a suitable strip for each group plus a few extra ones for those groups who finish quickly. Also ensure that each group has access to a supply of multilink cubes to continue the patterns.

Resources
Multilink cubes, 2cm squared paper, colouring materials.

What to do
Introduction
Hold up a strip of about six multilink cubes that form a simple repeating pattern, for example red, blue, red, blue, red, blue. Ask the children whether there is anything special about the strip of cubes. Provide further prompts if necessary, such as: *What do you notice about the colours of the cubes?* Ask pupils to explain the pattern in their own words. Point to one end of the strip and ask what colour comes next. Select a child to come out and attach the appropriate cube to the strip. Repeat this several times and ensure that the children are introduced to the expression 'repeating pattern'.

Hold up another strip of cubes that form a more complex pattern, for example black, white, white, red, black, white, white, red. Again, encourage the children to talk about the pattern in their own words and ask individuals to come out and attach additional cubes in order to continue the pattern.

The possible examples that can be used here are limitless. Make the patterns as simple or as complex as you wish according to the ability of the pupils.

Main activity

Organize pupils into small groups of three or four, according to ability. Give each group a supply of multilink cubes in a variety of colours. Provide one child in each group with a strip of multilink cubes that form a repeating pattern. He or she must continue the pattern by adding one cube to the strip. It is then passed on to the next child who also adds a cube. The strip is passed around the group until everyone has added two or three cubes. The children must then record the repeating pattern by shading squares on 2cm squared paper in the same colours. (This type of paper is ideal because the squares are the same size as the faces of the cubes although it is possible to use paper with smaller squares.)

Circulate around the groups while the children are working, watching out for errors in the repeating patterns. Pick up on any errors by asking appropriate questions and prompts, for example: *Call out the colours in your sequence* and *Are you sure the last one should be red?*

When the children have recorded the repeating pattern, provide the group with another starting strip or alternatively ask one of the children to make a starting strip of their own for the group to work with.

Plenary

Hold up some of the children's drawings and ask the rest of the class to describe the pattern and say what cubes come next. Choose patterns of increasing complexity. Use this time to ask the children if they have seen repeating patterns elsewhere, for example around the school, outside or at home. Possible examples include fabrics, wallpaper, tiles and various borders. Show children one or two examples of these repeating patterns if you have them available. Ask them to look for a repeating pattern at home, draw it and bring it in to school.

Suggestion(s) for extension

Provide increasingly complex patterns for the children to continue, particularly the more able children, for example:

The patterns can also be based on position as well as colour, for example:

Suggestion(s) for support

Less able children can work with simple patterns appropriate to their ability. Some children could also do this as a purely practical activity without the recording.

Assessment opportunities

By observing the children while they add cubes to the strips you will be able to judge whether or not they are able to identify a repeating pattern. Their drawings will also provide valuable evidence of this.

Opportunities for IT

Many drawing programs include a selection of pre-drawn 'stamps' which can be pasted onto the screen. These can be used to demonstrate repeating patterns. Children could also produce their own repeating pattern and print it out.

Display ideas

Use the children's drawings of the repeating patterns to create an attractive wall display.

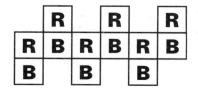

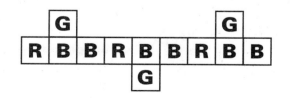

100-SQUARE JIGSAWS

To recognize the number patterns that exist within a 100 square.

†† *Whole-class introduction followed by work in pairs and whole-class plenary.*

🕐 *Introduction 10–15 minutes; main activity 30–35 minutes; plenary 5–10 minutes; total 45–60 minutes.*

Previous skills/knowledge needed

Children should be familiar with numbers up to 100 although it is possible to adapt the activity for those who are not familiar with such large numbers as described in the 'Suggestion(s) for support' section below. Some questions posed during the introduction require pupils to understand the concept of left and right.

Key background information

Children need to be aware of the patterns that exist in our number system in order to carry out mental arithmetic efficiently and effectively. A 100-square is a valuable resource when looking at simple number patterns.

Preparation

Make copies of photocopiable pages 110 and 111 onto card so that each pair has a copy of both sheets. It is a good idea to use card in a variety of colours so that pairs working close to one another do not get their jigsaw pieces mixed up. Ensure that scissors (ideally one pair per pupil) and glue are available. Make copies of photocopiable page 112 on to card for children who go on to do the extension activity.

Resources

Large poster-size 100-square, photocopiable pages 110, 111 and 112, scissors, glue, sheets of blank A4 paper or card, pencils. For the extension activity – 2cm squared paper/blank 10 × 10 grids.

What to do

Introduction

Using a large poster-size 100-square as a visual aid, ask the children questions about the number patterns they can see, for example: *What is special about the way the numbers are arranged? What happens to the numbers as we move across this way? What happens as we move down this way?*

Cover up individual numbers or blocks of numbers and ask the children to tell you what they are. You could also tell pupils to close their eyes (or cover up the 100-square so that they cannot see it) and ask questions such as: *Which number is to the right of 12? Which number is above 27? Which number is underneath 39?* and so on.

Main activity

Cover up the large 100-square so that the children cannot refer to it during the main activity. Organize the children into pairs and hand out the copies of photocopiable pages 110 and 111. Explain that the children must cut out the jigsaw pieces and reassemble them to make a 100-square. When the jigsaw is complete the pieces can be stuck onto a blank sheet of paper or card.

Using a copy of photocopiable page 112, children can also produce their own 100-square jigsaw and then pass it on to another child to complete. You can either specify the number of pieces the jigsaw must comprise according to ability or alternatively allow the children to decide themselves. The grid-lines on the photocopiable sheet are dotted so that the child creating the jigsaw can easily draw over these to identify the outline of each piece. When they are happy with their pieces they can cut them out and hand them over to another child to piece together.

Plenary

Use the plenary to ask further questions about the patterns in a 100-square. Again, ensure that pupils cannot refer to a 100-square anywhere in the room. Ask questions such as: *If I start at 25 and move one square to the right and one square down where do I end up?*

Suggestion(s) for extension

When producing their own 100-square jigsaw, children could start by filling in their own 100-square rather than using the one provided on photocopiable page 112. They could use a sheet of 2cm squared paper or a blank 10 × 10 grid. You could specify the way that the 100-square should be filled in, for example you might ask them to fill it in one column at a time or fill it in one diagonal at a time. They will need to think carefully about the number patterns in a 100-square.

Suggestion(s) for support

Photocopiable pages 110 and 111 provide a jigsaw with 15 pieces. If you feel that this is not suitable for some children then use photocopiable page 112 to produce a jigsaw with fewer pieces. Cut out the pieces, spread them out over two sheets, and stick the pieces down to produce your own photocopiable version of the jigsaw.

Another possibility is to use only the top half of a 100 square, that is, the numbers 1–50.

Assessment opportunities
The children's responses during the introduction and plenary will indicate whether or not they understand the patterns that exist in a 100-square.

Display ideas
The children's own jigsaws, both assembled and unassembled, can be used to produce an interesting wall display.

Reference to photocopiable sheets
Photocopiable pages 110 and 111 provide jigsaw-shaped pieces of a 100-square which the children have to cut out and reassemble. Photocopiable page 112 provides a complete 100-square. The children can cut this up and create their own puzzle. Alternatively, it can be adapted for use with less able children.

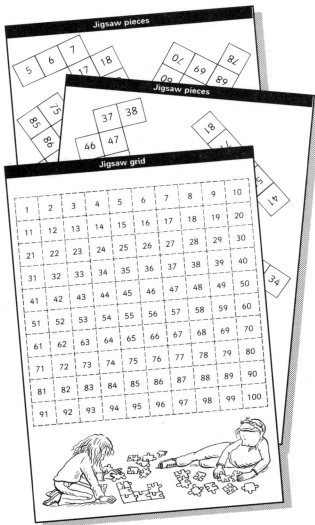

NUMBER NECKLACES

To generate number sequences using the constant function of a calculator. To recognize and continue number sequences.

†† *Whole-class introduction followed by work in pairs and whole-class plenary.*

⏱ *Introduction 10–15 minutes; main activity 20–25; plenary 15–20 minutes; total 45–60 minutes.*

Previous skills/knowledge needed
Children should be familiar with numbers up to 100 although it is possible for them to work with smaller numbers. They will also need to have done some work on pattern, starting with visual patterns and moving on to simple number patterns. The previous two activities focus on these areas.

Key background information
An awareness of pattern within our number system lies at the heart of sound arithmetic skills. This activity builds on earlier pattern work. It requires pupils to not only be aware of and identify patterns, but also to continue them. The activity also makes use of a powerful calculator facility, the constant function, first introduced in the activity 'Fast fingers' on page 20.

Preparation
Make copies of photocopiable page 113 so that there is at least one copy per pupil. (This can be enlarged or reduced to make it appropriate for the needs of individual pupils.) Also ensure that there are enough calculators, one per pupil. Investigate how the constant function operates on the calculators you are using. In most cases you need to press:

But on some older calculators it is:

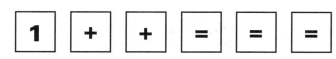

Resources
Calculators, photocopiable page 113, writing materials, paper, board/flip chart.

What to do
Introduction
If the children are already familiar with the constant function then recap this by asking questions such as: *What happens when we press 1+= = = =?* If they are not familiar with this then talk them through the key presses described above and let them explore and discuss the facility.

Next, ask pupils what they think will happen if they press 2 + = = =. Some children should be capable of working this out. They might describe it in a number of different ways, for example 'counting in 2s', 'even numbers', 'you miss out a number', 'numbers in the two times table', and so on. Use this as an opportunity to explore some of these concepts. Draw a necklace shape on the board and write in the first few numbers in the sequence. Like this:

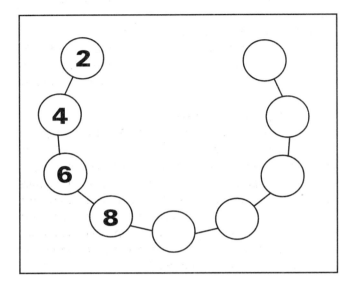

Tell the children to put their calculators down and then ask them to tell you what the next few numbers in the sequence will be in order to complete the necklace.

Try this again, for example using 5 + = = = or 7 + = = =. Again, ask the children to explain the sequence in their own words. Write the first few numbers in the sequence on the board and then ask pupils to work out the next few numbers without using their calculators.

Main activity

Organize the children into pairs, ideally with someone of similar ability, and give each child a copy of photocopiable page 113. Explain that each pupil must use the constant function to produce the first four numbers of a sequence. These numbers should then be written into the first four beads of a necklace on the photocopiable sheet. The children should then swap their 'necklaces' and complete their partner's pattern without using a calculator. This can be repeated several times, using additional copies of the photocopiable sheet if necessary.

Plenary

Ask individual children to read out the first four or five numbers on their necklaces. Then ask others in the class to say what the next four or five numbers will be. Repeat this several times.

Use the plenary to consider more complex sequences. Call out (or write on the board) the first four or five numbers of a decreasing sequence, for example 30, 28, 26, 24, 22,

and ask the children to say what the next four or five numbers will be. You could also use sequences that are not multiples, for example counting in 3s starting with 2 (2, 5, 8, 11, 14 …). As in the introduction, always ask pupils to explain the sequences in their own words.

Suggestion(s) for extension

Children could be shown how to use the constant function to generate some of the more complex sequences described above and then incorporate such sequences into their main activity.

For most calculators a decreasing sequence (30, 28, 26, 24 …) is obtained by pressing:

A sequence such as 2, 5, 8, 11, 14 is usually obtained by pressing:

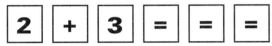

Suggestion(s) for support

You may like to work with a group of less able pupils during the main activity. Show them how to generate some of the fairly straightforward sequences used during the introduction, for example counting in 2s. Tell them to press the equals key just once and then ask: *What comes next?*

Tell them to press the equals key once more to see if they were correct and then ask again: *What comes next?* See how far they can go. A number line or a large 100-square are useful aids. Repeat this with other sequences, for example counting in 3s, 4s or 5s. Children should eventually be able to move on to do the same main activity as the rest of the class, working in pairs.

Assessment opportunities

Working with a less able group during the main activity will give you an insight into whether or not they are beginning to understand simple number sequences. The written work provided by the rest of the class will provide valuable evidence.

Opportunities for IT

It is important that children are able to use effectively the facilities of an electronic calculator such as the constant function. This activity provides an opportunity to develop such skills.

Display ideas

The children's completed number necklaces can be used to produce a classroom display.

Reference to photocopiable sheet

Photocopiable page 113 provides a number of blank necklace shapes into which the children write the beginnings of a number pattern. The sheet is then passed onto a partner for him or her to complete.

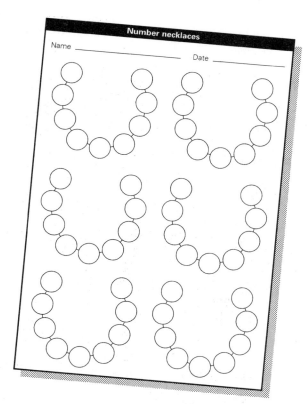

SHADING PATTERNS

To identify and continue visual and numerical patterns in a 100-square. To practise mental counting-on skills.

†† *Whole-class introduction followed by work in pairs and whole-class plenary.*

🕐 *Introduction 10–15 minutes; main activity 20–25; plenary 15–20 minutes; total 45–60 minutes.*

Previous skills/knowledge needed

Children will need to be familiar with numbers up to 100 and should have done some work on pattern, starting with visual patterns and moving on to simple number patterns.

Key background information

This activity is similar to 'Number necklaces' on page 41 in that it utilizes the constant function on a calculator to generate simple number sequences and then asks pupils to identify the patterns and continue them. The difference here is that by using a partially completed 100-square children can consider the patterns in both visual and numerical terms. You might prefer pupils to use mental counting-on skills to generate the number sequences rather than the constant function.

Preparation

Ensure that there are enough calculators for one per pupil and investigate how the constant function operates (see 'Number necklaces' on page 41). Make copies of photocopiable page 114 so that there is at least one sheet per pupil. It is likely that some children will need more than one so ensure that there are a few extra copies. Also make an enlarged copy for demonstration with the class. Attach it to the wall, board or easel so that all the children can see it. Also make copies of photocopiable page 115 for the extension activities. Additional enlarged grids are required during the plenary.

Resources

Photocopiable pages 114 and 115, an enlarged copy of photocopiable page 114, one calculator per pupil, pencils or crayons, board/flip chart.

What to do

Introduction

If the children have already used the constant function in activities such as 'Fast fingers' or 'Number necklaces' then recap on this work by asking questions such as: *Can you remember what happens when we press 1 + = = = = ?* and *What happens when we press 3 + = = = = ?* If the children are not familiar with the constant function then you will need to talk them through the key presses and let them explore and discuss the facility.

Tell the pupils to use the constant function to count in

3s or 4s. After each count shade in the appropriate number on your enlarged copy of the 100-square or allow one of the children to do the shading. You may like to ask pupils to predict what the next number will be before they press the equals key. Keep counting and shading until you get to the end of the fifth row in the 100-square, that is, only shade the top half which contains numbers.

Tell the children to look carefully at the shading and ask them to explain what they can see. Then, without using calculators, pupils should come out one at a time and shade the next square in the pattern. You can get them to work from left to right across each row but you could also look at the visual pattern as you work down each column. When all the shading is complete you could quickly write in the first few rows of numbers beyond 50 and the pupils can use the constant function again to check whether the shadings are correct.

Main activity

Arrange the class into pairs and hand out one copy of photocopiable page 114 to each child. Tell the children to use the constant function to generate a number sequence. They should then shade in the appropriate numbers in the top half of their 100-square. (You could specify the amount that each pupil must count in by telling them or by writing it on their sheet in advance. In this way you can match the task to the ability of individual pupils.) Tell the children that when they have shaded the top half they must swap the sheet with their partner who must then complete the shading without the use of a calculator. Finally, they can write in the numbers 51–100 and use the constant function to check whether their shadings are correct.

This process can be repeated several times. By using different colours it is possible to shade more than one sequence on a single 100-square and so reduce photocopying costs. In this case pupils should not write in

the numbers 51–100 until both sequences have been shaded completely.

Plenary

Use this time to introduce and explore some of the activities described below and on the opposite page. On the board or a large piece of paper draw a large grid like the one shown here.

1	2	3	4	5	6	7	8	9
10	11	12	13	14	15	16	17	18
19	20	21	22	23	24	25	26	27
28	29	30	31	32	33	34	35	36

Start by asking pupils to talk about the grid. You could ask questions such as: *Is this the same as the 100-squares you have been using?* and *In what ways is it different?* Without using calculators ask the class, either individually or collectively to count in 2s, starting with 2. Shade in the appropriate numbers on the grid or ask pupils to come out and do the shading. Discuss the visual pattern and continue the shading in the bottom half of the grid.

Next, compare this counting in 2s pattern with the

counting in 2s pattern on a 100-square. Ask a child who has done the latter during the main activity to hold up his or her work for everyone to see. Ask pupils to describe the two different patterns (one is a chequered pattern, the other is stripy).

Show the pupils a large version of this grid.

1	2	3	4	5	6	7	8
9	10	11	12	13	14	15	16
17	18	19	20	21	22	23	24
25	26	27	28	29	30	31	32
33	34	35	36	37	38	39	40

Tell the children that you are going to count in 2s again and shade in the numbers. Ask them what they think the pattern will look like; will it be chequered or stripy or neither of these? Encourage pupils to give reasons for their answers. Finally, do the counting and shading to see whether they were right. Some pupils might be capable of generalizing this situation (for instance, stripy patterns for even widths of grid, chequered patterns for odd widths) and so you could bring this out in your discussions.

Suggestion(s) for extension

After they have used a 100-square a few times, give children the grids shown on photocopiable page 115. Explain that the procedure is the same as when using a 100-square. (The children are generating their own number sequences.) You could ask them to predict what the patterns will look like before they start shading.

Suggestion(s) for support

Less able children can use simpler patterns, for example counting in 2s, 5s and 10s.

Assessment opportunities

Watch pupils as they shade the bottom half of the 100-square. Ask them to explain the pattern and how they know which squares to shade. This, together with the completed photocopiable sheets, will indicate whether or not they are capable of identifying and continuing patterns.

Opportunities for IT

The program *Multiple* produced by MicroSMILE generates number grids to your own specification and allows you to shade multiples of your choice. You could use this program to demonstrate quickly some of the patterns and let pupils check their answers. It is available for BBC, RM Nimbus PC-186, Archimedes and Windows-based computers.

Reference to photocopiable sheets

Photocopiable page 114 has two 100-squares which the children have to shade and complete using different number sequences. Photocopiable page 115 provides varying number grids to extend the children's work.

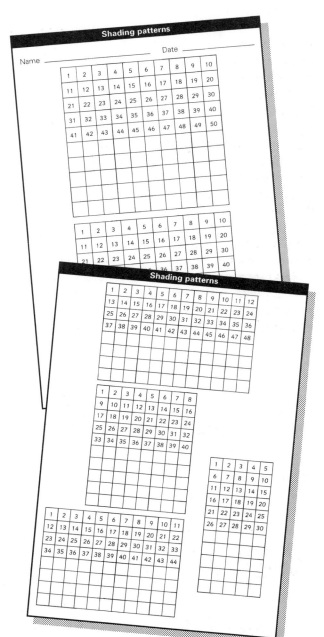

STARS AND SHAPES

To mentally produce number sequences based on multiples. To use number sequences to produce visual patterns. To recognize similarities and differences in visual patterns.

†† *Whole-class introduction followed by individual work and whole-class plenary.*

⏱ *Introduction 10–15 minutes; main activity 20–25 minutes; plenary 15–20 minutes; total 45–60 minutes.*

Previous skills/knowledge needed

Children will need to be familiar with numbers up to 100 and have done some pattern work, both visual and numerical. They will also need to be able to draw straight lines with a pencil and ruler.

Key background information

This activity uses simple number sequences to generate visual patterns on a clock-face numbered 0–9. Children can produce the sequences using mental counting-on skills or alternatively generate them using the constant function on a calculator. The latter can be justified since two of the learning objectives above are concerned with pattern. Five different visual patterns are produced depending on the number sequence used; a decagon (counting in 1s or 9s), a pentagon (counting in 2s or 8s), a 10-pointed star (counting in 3s or 7s), a 5-pointed star (counting in 4s or 6s) and a horizontal line (counting in 5s).

Preparation

Make copies of photocopiable page 116, one for each child. Many children will need more than one so ensure there are a few extra copies. Some children might also benefit from using an enlarged version. Draw a copy of the numbered clock-face on the board or on a large sheet of paper. You will need this during the introduction when explaining how to draw the patterns.

Resources

Photocopiable page 116, pencils, rulers, paper, board/flip chart.

What to do

Introduction

Ask the children to slowly count in 3s starting with 3, either collectively or on an individual basis. Count at least as far as 36 and list the numbers on the board as pupils call them out. You might like to use this as an opportunity to introduce or recap the word 'multiple'. Then introduce pupils to the clock-face and ask them to talk about it by asking questions such as: *Is this a normal clock face? What is different about it?* and so on. Demonstrate how to draw a pattern on the clock-face using the multiples of 3 which

are listed on the board. Start at 3 and then draw a straight line from there to the second number, 6. Then draw a line from the 6 to the 9. Explain that with the next number, 12, we use only the units digit and so draw a line from 9 to 2. The next line is from 2 to 5 (for 15), the next is from 5 to 8 (for 18) and so on. Keep going until you get back to the starting point, 3. This should produce a 10-pointed star. Ask the children to describe the pattern in their own words.

Main activity

Tell the children to choose a number from 1–9 and then list the multiples of that number. Alternatively, they could generate the multiples using the constant function on a calculator. Using the list of multiples, they should then draw a pattern on one of the clock faces on photocopiable page 116. Pupils can repeat this until they have used multiples of all the numbers from 1–9.

Ask those children who complete all nine patterns to look at them carefully and see how many different ones there are. Also ask them to find out which numbers produce the same pattern. They could describe these things in their own words on the reverse side of the photocopiable sheet.

Plenary

Start by giving pupils an opportunity to hold up their work to show the rest of the class. You may like to work through each set of multiples in turn and perhaps display the pattern for each one on the wall and label it. Next, ask the pupils how many different patterns they can see and which ones are the same. Most pupils should be able to spot the matching pairs of patterns and some might notice that those which match use multiples of numbers which always add up to ten (so the patterns for 1 and 9 are the same, as are the patterns for 2 and 8, 3 and 7, 4 and 6).

Suggestion(s) for extension

Some pupils might like to use multiples of numbers greater than 10. Again, it is always the units digit which is used when drawing the pattern. Ask them to investigate whether any new patterns are produced (only the original five patterns will be produced).

Suggestion(s) for support

Less able pupils might need a lot of help with the drawing aspect of the work and so you might need to spend much of your time with one group. Problems with the arithmetic can be overcome by letting them use the constant function of a calculator or restricting them to multiples of easier numbers such as 2 and 5.

Assessment opportunities

The children's completed photocopiable sheets will provide a wide range of assessment evidence. Observe their ability to mentally count on or work out multiples, their ability to use a pencil and ruler effectively, and their ability to match pairs of patterns. Also, during the plenary, make a note of those pupils who are able to explain that the matching patterns use multiples of numbers that always add up to 10.

Opportunities for IT

The program *Circle* produced by MicroSMILE explores a similar theme to the one in this activity. You specify the number of points on the circle and how they are to be joined. The program can be used as a starting point for several pieces of investigative work, with children working at the computer themselves or alternatively it can be used to demonstrate key points. The program is available for BBC, RM Nimbus PC-186, Archimedes and Windows-based computers.

Display ideas

The completed patterns can be mounted, labelled and used to produce an attractive classroom display.

Reference to photocopiable sheet

Photocopiable page 116 provides a number of blank clock-faces. Using multiples of different numbers, the children create varying patterns.

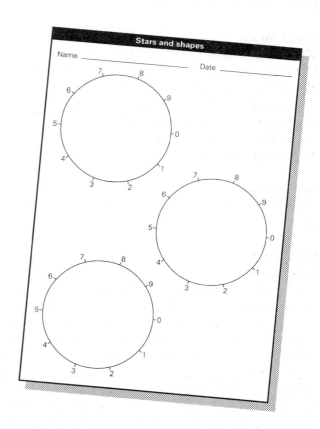

DOTTY SEQUENCES

To identify numbers which belong to a particular set or sequence. To continue these number sequences.

†† *Whole class introduction followed by individual work and whole-class plenary.*

⊕ *Introduction 10–15 minutes; main activity 20–25 minutes; plenary 15–20 minutes; total 45–60 minutes.*

Previous skills/knowledge needed

Children will need to be familiar with numbers up to 100 and have some experience of simple number patterns involving counting on, multiples, odd numbers, even numbers, and so on.

Key background information

This activity provides further valuable practice at spotting and continuing simple number sequences. These are important skills and so pupils need to develop them in a wide range of situations.

Preparation

Make copies of photocopiable page 117, one for each child. (Some pupils might benefit from using an enlarged version of the photocopiable sheet.) On the board write all of the numbers from 1–20. Position these at random all over the board and mark a dot at the side of each one so that the board resembles a dot-to-dot puzzle.

Resources

Photocopiable page 117, rulers, writing materials, board/ flip chart, different coloured chalks or marker pens.

What to do

Introduction

Recap earlier work on simple number sequences based on counting on, odd numbers, even numbers and so on. These can be 'chanted' by the whole group or you could ask individuals to give you the next number in the sequence. You might want to use this as an opportunity to introduce the word 'multiple' and you could also introduce unusual sequences, for example counting in 3s starting at 2.

After recapping several sequences, turn to the board and explain that you are going to do a dot-to-dot puzzle using number sequences. Ask a child to pick a sequence of their own choice. As individuals call out each number in the sequence, join the corresponding numbers with straight lines. For example, if the sequence is counting in 4s starting with 4 then you will join 4 to 8, 8 to 12, 12 to 16, and 16 to 20. Repeat this with another sequence, perhaps using a different colour for the lines. Point out that some numbers may be used in more than one sequence and that this is perfectly acceptable.

Main activity

Give out a copy of photocopiable page 117 to each child and ask them to complete the dot-to-dot puzzles. They should use a pencil and ruler to join the numbers in each of the sequences listed on the sheet. This should form a simple drawing.

Children who finish early can write down the numbers in each sequence on the reverse side of their photocopiable sheet and then continue each sequence by writing down the next five numbers.

Plenary

First use this as an opportunity to hold up and praise children's work. Ask questions about the completed photocopiable sheets, for example: *Were there any numbers that appeared in more than one sequence? Which number was used the most?* and so on.

Finally, get pupils to think about number sequences in a slightly different way. Write a number on the board, for

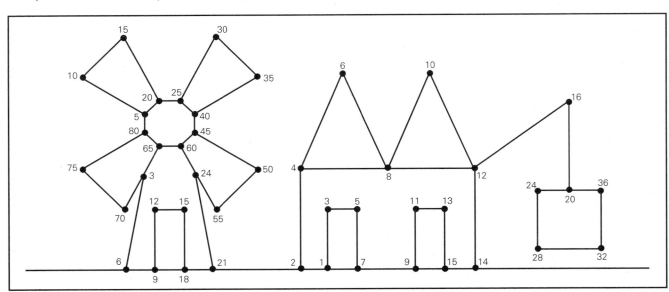

example 24. Ask the children to think of and then describe a number sequence that includes 24. Other pupils can call out the numbers in the sequence to see whether it does include 24. Then ask for another sequence that also includes 24. This can be repeated several times with 24 before moving on to a new number.

Suggestion(s) for extension

Children who complete the task quickly can design and produce a similar sheet of their own and then pass it on to another pupil to complete.

Suggestion(s) for support

Some children might need help with the drawing as well as the number sequences and so these children may require extra attention. Problems with the number sequences can be overcome by giving pupils access to a number line or a 100-square. Another option is to let them use the constant function of a calculator.

Assessment opportunities

The children's completed photocopiable sheets will give an indication of whether or not they are able to identify numbers which belong to a particular sequence. Evidence of being able to continue a sequence will be available on the reverse side of the sheet.

Reference to photocopiable sheet

Photocopiable page 117 shows numbers in the range 1–80 laid out around the page. Following the number sequences listed on the sheet, the children have to join the numbers to create a simple picture.

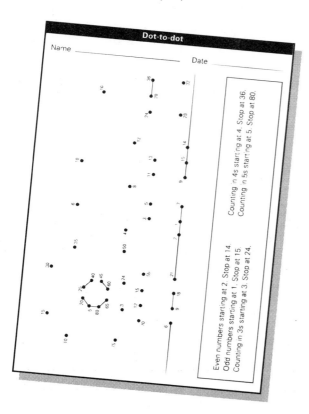

MULTILINK SEQUENCES

To recognize and continue a visual sequence produced using practical apparatus. To identify numerical patterns associated with a visual sequence.

†† *Whole-class introduction followed by group-work and whole-class plenary.*

⏱ *Introduction 10–15 minutes; main activity 20–25 minutes; plenary 15–20 minutes; total 45–60 minutes.*

Previous skills/knowledge needed

Children will need to have had some experience of looking at and investigating pattern, both visual and numerical. They will also need to have an understanding of the use of ordinal numbers to denote position in a sequence.

Key background information

This activity is based on sequences of shapes made out of multilink cubes. There are many possible sequences that can be used, for example:

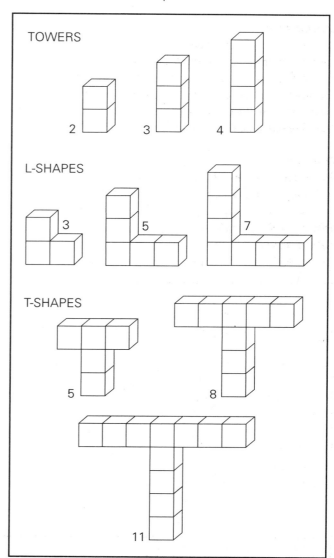

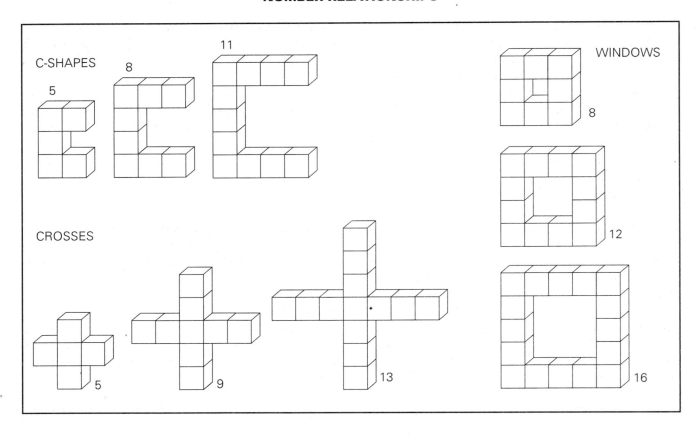

You will also be able to think of others.

This activity requires children to identify and continue sequences such as these by considering them in purely visual terms. They must then investigate the numerical sequences which exist. This lays a firm foundation for much of the algebra work required at Key Stage Two.

Preparation

During the main activity, each group will need to use several sets of shapes made from multilink cubes like the ones shown above and on page 49. Each set should comprise the first three shapes in a particular sequence. If possible, use the same colour of cubes for each shape in the sequence to avoid shapes from different sequences getting mixed up. The sets of shapes can circulate around the groups during the main activity so that two or three sets per group should be sufficient.

Resources

Sets of multilink shapes as described above, a supply of multilink cubes for each group, 2cm squared paper, coloured pencils or crayons, board/flip chart.

What to do

Introduction

Choose one of the fairly straightforward sets of shapes you have prepared in advance, for example the towers, and stand them up in order so that all the children can see them. Tell the pupils that these are multilink towers. Point to the smallest tower and say: *This is the first tower.*

Identify the other two towers in a similar fashion. Ask the pupils if they know what the fourth tower should look like. Let one of them make the next tower in the sequence. Similarly, get individual pupils to describe and then make the fifth and sixth towers.

Repeat this process with one of the more difficult sets of shapes, for example the windows. Remember to ask pupils to explain and justify their answers and pick up on any errors or misconceptions.

Main activity

Give each group a set of three shapes and tell them that they must make the next three shapes in the sequence. (Distribute the sets of shapes according to the ability of the pupils in each group.) All six shapes should then be recorded on a sheet of 2cm squared paper. As the pupils work, circulate around the groups, swapping their sets of three shapes for a new set as they complete each sequence.

When you feel that a particular group has had sufficient experience of continuing and recording these visual sequences, ask them to investigate the numerical sequences. For each sequence they must list the number of cubes used in each shape and explain the number sequence in their own words. They could also write down the next three or four numbers in the sequence.

Plenary

Use this time as an opportunity for pupils to present and explain their answers. Choose a sequence, hold up the first three shapes, and then ask children to hold up their sketches of the next three shapes or get them to quickly make them from multilink. List the number of cubes used in each shape on the board and ask pupils to explain the pattern and give the next three or four numbers.

This can be repeated for several different sets of shapes, gradually increasing the level of difficulty. As you are working, reinforce and discuss language associated with these sequences, for example the 'L' shapes produce a sequence of odd numbers and the square windows produce multiples of 4.

Suggestion(s) for extension

Children who cope well with this activity can use more challenging sets of shapes such as those shown below. In these examples the numbers do not increase by a constant amount as you work through the sequence.

Suggestion(s) for support

Less able pupils need use only the easier sets of shapes and work in purely visual terms rather than consider the numerical sequences.

Assessment opportunities

This activity should provide a valuable insight into the children's abilities to spot and continue patterns at various levels. The least able children will probably be able to physically make shapes that follow a simple sequence. Other children will be able to record these shapes on paper, while others will be able to spot and continue the associated numerical sequences. The most able children will be able to work with complex sequences such as those shown below.

Opportunities for IT

The number sequences can be entered onto a spreadsheet and shown in graphical form. This would illustrate how the number of cubes in each shape increases at a steady rate.

Display ideas

The sequences of multilink shapes can be used to form a table-top display, which could be complemented by some of the children's sketches of the shapes displayed on the wall.

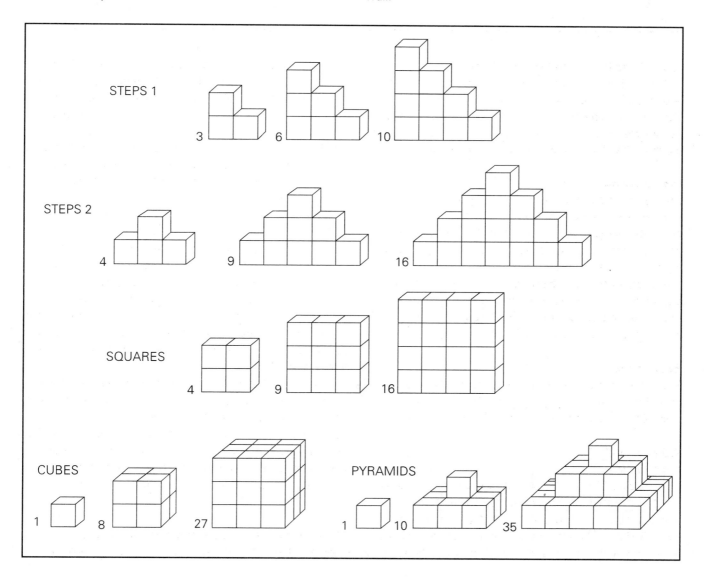

HUNT THE DOMINO

To identify a missing item from a set by using various sorting and ordering strategies.

†† *Whole-class introduction followed by group-work and whole-class plenary.*

⏱ *Introduction 10–15 minutes; main activity 15–20 minutes; plenary 10–15 minutes; total 35–50 minutes.*

Previous skills/knowledge needed

Children will need to have had some experience of early sorting, matching and ordering activities, using a wide range of attributes.

Key background information

In this open-ended problem-solving activity children work in groups to ascertain which domino has been removed from a normal set. They are free to choose their own strategies but these are likely to involve ordering and sorting based on visual features (for instance, arrangements of spots) as well as on number.

Preparation

Draw a rectangle on the board and write in it the numbers 1–10, randomly scattered. Miss out one of the numbers (not 1 or 10). An alternative is to write the numbers on a large sheet of paper. Repeat this for the letters A–H, again omitting one of the letters (not A or H). Do this again for the seven days of the week, missing out any one of the days. Also ensure that there is one set of dominoes for each group of pupils and remove one domino from each

set (not necessarily the same domino each time). If you do not have sufficient sets of dominoes then use photocopiable page 118. Make copies of the sheet onto card, using a variety of colours so that children do not mix up the resulting sets of dominoes.

Resources

One set of dominoes per group (use photocopiable page 118 if necessary), board/flip chart.

What to do

Introduction

Point to the rectangle containing the numbers 1–10 (or hold up the sheet of paper). Ask the children to work out what is wrong with these numbers. When someone has spotted that there is a number missing, ask the child to explain how he or she worked it out. Repeat this for the letters and the days of the week, again asking pupils to explain how they did it.

Tell children that they are going to solve more problems like this using a set of dominoes. Introduce the dominoes by asking questions about them such as: *Does anyone know what dominoes look like? What numbers of spots do you see on a domino? Which domino will have the biggest number of spots? Which one will have the fewest spots? How many dominoes will have three spots on one half?* and so on.

Main activity

Give each group one set of dominoes (use the photocopiable sheet, if necessary). Explain to the children that this set of dominoes has one domino missing and

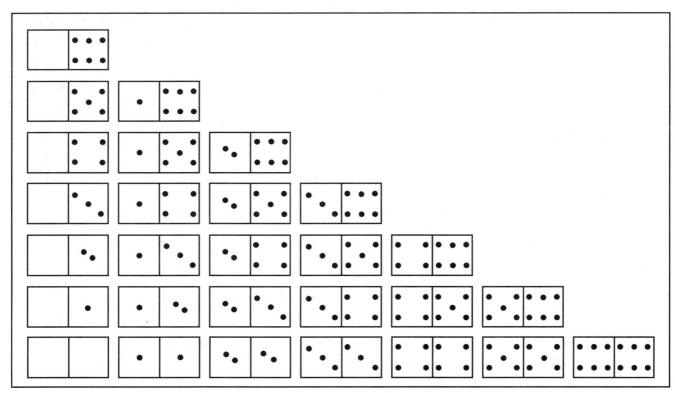

that they have to work out which one it is.

Circulate around the groups and observe the way they tackle the problem. Ask them questions about the approaches they are using, for example: *Why are you arranging the dominoes like that?* When a group thinks they know which domino is missing, ask them to explain how they worked out the answer. If they are correct you could replace the missing domino, randomly remove another one and so repeat the whole process.

It is possible to add a competitive element to this activity if you feel that this is appropriate, seeing who can find the missing domino the quickest.

Plenary

Ask children to explain the approaches they used to find the missing domino, particularly the ways in which they sorted, ordered or set them out. Either draw on the board or use actual dominoes as a visual aid during these discussions. This should lead to a consideration of the patterns that exist in the set. For example, you could start by asking pupils to list, in order, the dominoes which have a blank half. Then ask them to list those which have a single spot on one of the halves, two spots on one of the halves, three spots on one of the halves, and so on. In this way you will produce the pattern on the opposite page.

Suggestion(s) for extension

Ask those children with the necessary language and writing skills to provide a written description of how they found the missing domino.

Suggestion(s) for support

Less able pupils could use a restricted set of dominoes, for example you could leave out any dominoes with five or six spots on one half. This will result in a set of fifteen dominoes, from which you will remove one.

If children have not laid out the dominoes in some sort of order when tackling the problem, then ask them to do this as a follow-up activity. Simply ask them to set out the dominoes in order so that they can see them all clearly.

Assessment opportunities

Observe the approaches used during the main activity. This will give an indication of the children's awareness of pattern and their ability to use it to solve problems. Some children might simply go in search of a particular domino, find it, search for another until they find it, and so on. Others will approach the task in a more logical manner based on pattern and order.

Display ideas

The diagram on page 52 shows one possible way to sort a set of dominoes but there are other possibilities that pupils may find for themselves during the main activity. These would make a valuable classroom display.

Reference to photocopiable sheet

If you do not have sufficient sets of wooden or plastic dominoes then make sets by copying photocopiable page 118 on to card. Use a different colour of card for each set so that the dominoes do not get mixed up.

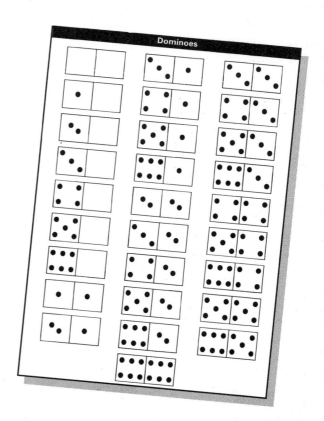

ODD AND EVEN WITH DOMINOES

To identify odd and even numbers. To spot patterns and relationships when odd and even numbers are combined.

†† *Whole-class introduction followed by individual work and whole-class plenary.*

⏱ *Introduction 10–15 minutes; main activity 20–25 minutes; plenary 15–20 minutes; total 45–60 minutes.*

Previous skills/knowledge needed

Children will need to be familiar with numbers up to 12 and have been introduced to the concept of odd and even numbers.

Key background information

This activity gives children practice at identifying odd and even numbers but the main aim is for them to spot the patterns and relationships that exist when odd and even numbers are combined (added). Many pupils should be capable of spotting that when they combine an odd number with an odd number the result is an even number, when they combine an even number with an even number the result is an even number, and when they combine an odd number with an even number the result is an odd number.

Preparation

Make copies of photocopiable page 118, one for each child. Reproduce the two diagrams shown below, each one on a large sheet of paper.

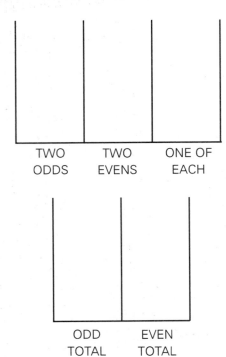

Resources

Photocopiable page 118, scissors, coloured pencils or crayons, Blu-Tack, board/flip chart.

What to do

Introduction

Start by recapping earlier work on odd and even numbers. You could do this by writing a selection of numbers on the board and asking children to pick out those which are odd and those which are even. Alternatively, ask the children to give you examples of odd and even numbers and to explain how they can tell whether a number is odd or even. When children are first introduced to the concept of odd and even numbers it is often explained in terms of objects in a set having a partner, for example 7 is an odd number because if there were seven pupils not everyone would have a partner. More sophisticated explanations might be in terms of halving (even numbers can be halved without leaving a remainder) or the value of the units digit (even numbers always end in 0, 2, 4, 6 or 8).

Next, introduce the pupils to dominoes if they are not already familiar with them. Before showing them the dominoes ask questions about them such as: *Does anyone know what dominoes look like? What numbers of spots do you see on a domino? Which domino will have the biggest number of spots? Which one will have the fewest spots? How many dominoes will have three spots on one half?* and so on.

Then bring the two themes together. Hold up or draw a domino and ask whether the numbers on each half are odd or even. If the domino has one odd and one even number ask pupils for an example of a domino with two odd numbers and an example with two even numbers. One issue that might arise (and if it does not then raise it with a question) is whether zero (a blank) is odd or even. Let pupils explain their views on this. The conclusion you need to reach is that if we have to decide one way or the other then it ought to be even. This can be explained in terms of the way numbers alternate between odd and even as we count up or down in 1s.

Finally, reiterate that there are three types of domino: those with two odds, those with two evens and those with one of each. Ask the children which type they think occurs most often in a set of dominoes, or do they think there are roughly equal numbers of each? They can find out for themselves in the main activity.

Main activity

Distribute one copy of photocopiable page 118 to each child. The children should work individually on the photocopiable sheet using pencils or crayons in two colours, one corresponding to odd numbers and one to even numbers. Explain that they must shade the halves of each domino on the photocopiable sheet in the appropriate colour. Remind them that blanks are even.

As they finish the initial task, tell the children to cut out the dominoes and sort them into three piles: those with two odds, those with two evens and those with one of each. (They could write their name or initials on the back of each domino as they cut them out so that they do not get them mixed up with those belonging to other pupils sitting at the same table.)

The third task is to sort the dominoes into two piles: those with an odd number of spots on the whole domino and those with an even number. This important part of the main activity is discussed with pupils at length during the plenary.

Plenary

Discuss the findings of the main activity using one of the pupils' sets of shaded dominoes. Give children one shaded domino each (some might have to share, some may have more than one, depending on how many pupils there are in the class). Ask the children to come out in turn and stick their domino in to the appropriate column on the first large sheet of paper you prepared earlier (see 'Preparation').

Not only does this answer the question posed at the end of the introduction but it can also be used as a way of introducing or revising the idea of a block or bar graph.

Using another pupil's set of shaded dominoes, give out another domino to each child and again ask them to come out in turn and stick their domino in to the appropriate column on the second large sheet of paper you prepared earlier (see 'Preparation').

When the diagram is complete, ask the children what they notice about it. Some should spot that the first column contains only those dominoes whose two halves are shaded in different colours (one half is odd and the other is even) and the other contains only those whose two halves are shaded in the same colour (both halves are odd or both halves are even).

Suggestion(s) for extension

During the main activity, those children who spot the patterns and relationships when combining odd and even numbers could investigate this further using numbers greater than 6. Ask them to see whether it still works when we add any two numbers. They could also provide a written description of the relationship in their own words.

Suggestion(s) for support

Many parts of the main activity should be accessible to less able pupils, for example the shading and the sorting, possibly with the assistance of yourself or a classroom helper.

Assessment opportunities

The children's shadings will indicate their understanding of odd and even numbers. Also, observe pupils' data-handling skills when they are sorting their dominoes into three and then two piles. When pupils have sorted their dominoes into two piles ask them what they notice. This will provide an insight into their ability to spot the patterns and relationships that exist when combining odd and even numbers.

Opportunities for IT

The data produced in the main activity and discussed in the plenary could be entered into a data-handling package (for example, a spreadsheet) and used to produce two bar charts. These could be compared with the block graphs that were produced manually.

Display ideas

The two large block graphs produced during the plenary could form part of a valuable display focusing on odd and even numbers.

Reference to photocopiable sheet

Photocopiable page 118 provides a set of domino shapes. The children shade the odd and even dominoes in different colours and then sort them into various categories.

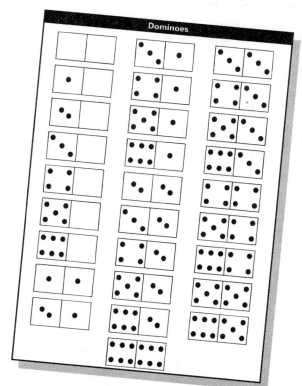

GO AND STAND WITH...

To decide whether or not a number belongs to a particular set. To identify the position of a number in a particular sequence. To practise mental arithmetic skills.

†† *Whole class activity in a large open space, for example the hall or playground.*

🕐 *Introduction 5–10 minutes; main activity 20–30 minutes; plenary 5 minutes; total 30–40 minutes.*

Previous skills/knowledge needed
Children should be familiar with numbers up to 100 and be aware of different types of numbers (odd and even numbers). They should also have some experience of simple number sequences and be able to carry out simple mental calculations.

Key background information
Children often think of maths as something that is only done sitting at a desk in a classroom. The activities presented here are accessible, enjoyable and provide a novel way of reinforcing several important number concepts.

Preparation
In this activity each child is numbered in an unbroken sequence starting with 1 (so, for example, if there are 30 pupils in the class then they will be numbered 1–30). Each pupil must wear a large label on their chest displaying their number. Prepare these in advance using sticky labels or use paper and sticky tape.

Resources
Number labels, one per pupil as described in 'Preparation'.

What to do
Introduction
Take the pupils to the hall or out to the playground. Explain that the main activities involve moving around and so stress that care needs to be taken. Reiterate any particular ground-rules or expectations you have with regard to movement, behaviour, and so on.

Explain that each pupil is going to be numbered. You could start by holding up one of the numbered labels towards you so that the children cannot see the number. Tell them that they must guess the number by asking questions to which you will reply 'yes' or 'no'. (See the activity 'Guess the number' on page 26 for further details of this type of activity.) When a child successfully guesses the number you can give them the label to stick on their chest. Repeat this several times, stopping occasionally to discuss good and bad choices of question. Encourage the pupils to guess the number using as few questions as possible.

After an appropriate number of turns, give out the remaining labels so that everybody has one.

Main activity
Explain to the children that you will be calling out instructions related to the numbers on their chests. They must listen to these carefully and then carry out the instructions when you say 'go'. Here is a selection of instructions you could give. You should be able to think of others yourself. After pupils have carried out each set of instructions remember to discuss and ask questions about any important points that crop up.

1. *When I say 'go' I want you to stand in a straight line in number order, smallest number at that side* (point), *biggest number at that side* (point).

This simple set of instructions is a good one to start with. Use it to ensure that all pupils know exactly what they have to do when you give instructions.

2. *When I say 'go' I want you to hold hands with the person whose number is one more than you.*

Some children might start to move away from their current position but in fact there is no need for anyone to move. They must simply hold hands with the pupil either side of them in the line, for example, 1 holds hands with 2, who holds hands with 3, and so on. The only child who will have a difficulty with this is the one with the highest number. Discuss this with the pupils when they have settled down.

3. When I say 'go' I want you to hold hands with the person whose number is two more than you.

This should produce two lines of pupils, one for odd numbers and one for even numbers (1 holds hands with 3, who holds hands with 5, and so on for the odd line, and 2 holds hands with 4, who holds hands with 6, and so on for the even line). The highest odd and highest even numbers will not be able to carry out the instructions. Discuss this and also ask the children what is special about the two lines, or what the numbers in each line are called.

4. When I say 'go' I want you to hold hands with the person whose number is three more than you.

This should produce three lines of pupils:

1, 4, 7, 10, …

2, 5, 8, 11, …

3, 6, 9, 12, …

You could point at the third line of these groups and ask: *What is special about these numbers? Where have we seen them before? What do we call them?* and so on.

Similarly you could ask children to hold hands with the person who is four more, five more, six more and so on. Some pupils might spot that these instructions produce, four, five and six lines respectively. Before saying 'go' for the last one you could ask pupils how many lines they think will be produced.

5. When I say 'go' I want you to hold hands with the person whose number is two less than you.

This produces two lines identical to those produced by the 'two more than you' instructions. Ask children if they have seen these two lines before and which other set of instructions produced them. Discuss why the two sets of instructions produce the same result.

This could be repeated using three less, four less, five less, and so on.

6. When I say 'go' I want you to stand with a partner so that your two numbers add up to 31.

Choose a total that is one more than the highest number, for example if there are 30 pupils then choose the number 31. This will result in 1 standing with 30, 2 with 28, and so on. If the number of pupils in the class is odd, for example 29, then there will always be someone without a partner (number 15 in this particular case). Ask questions about this such as: *There are 29 in the class. Why was there one person left without a partner?* and *Look at Andrew's number (15). Why could he not find a partner to make 30?*

7. Ask everyone to sit down. Then give instructions such as: *Stand up if your number is in the five times tables.* Check the numbers and pick up on any errors or misunderstandings. Ask those who have stood up to call out their numbers in ascending order. Ask the whole class to continue the sequence beyond 30.

Ask everyone to sit down again and repeat this for other times tables.

Plenary

Finish off by asking the children if they have enjoyed their maths lesson and asking them what they have learned from it.

Suggestion(s) for extension

Some of your questions could be directed at individuals rather than the whole class. For example, you could ask everyone to sit down and then say to an able pupil: *Go and find three people whose numbers add up to your own number.* Ensure that the able pupils have been allocated high numbers so that these sorts of questions pose a challenge.

SETS AND SEQUENCES

To identify numbers which belong to a particular set or sequence.

†† *Whole-class introduction followed by work in pairs or small groups and a whole-class plenary.*

🕐 *Introduction 5–10 minutes; main activity 20–25 minutes; plenary 5–10 minutes; total 30–45 minutes.*

Previous skills/knowledge needed

Most children will need to be familiar with numbers up to 100 and be aware of different types of numbers (odd and even numbers). They will also need to have some experience of simple number sequences and be able to carry out simple mental calculations.

Key background information

This activity provides another valuable opportunity for pupils to reinforce their knowledge of special sets of numbers and number sequences.

Preparation

Each pair or small group of pupils will need a set of 1–100 number cards. If you are making these yourself it would be best if you could use a variety of colours so that groups sitting close to one another do not get their sets mixed up. Also make two or three copies of photocopiable page 119 onto card and cut these up to form a pack of activity cards. The sets and sequences identified on the sheet are suitable for a wide range of ability. The easier ones are at the top of the sheet while the more challenging ones are at the bottom. You might be able to think of additional activity cards that can be added to the pack.

Resources

One pack of number cards per group, one pack of activity cards (made from photocopiable page 119), pencils, paper, board/flip chart.

What to do

Introduction

Start by recapping earlier work on special numbers (such as odd and even numbers, numbers in the times tables or multiples). You could do this by writing a selection of numbers on the board and asking children to pick out those that are odd, those that are even, those that are multiples of 3, and so on. Alternatively, ask pupils to give you examples of odd numbers, even numbers and multiples of 3. Also, recap earlier work on number sequences by writing the first few numbers of a sequence on the board and asking pupils to continue them. You could start with fairly straightforward examples (such as counting on in 3s starting at 3) and gradually move on to more challenging ones (counting on in 3s starting at 1 or 2).

Suggestion(s) for support

Walk among the pupils after you have called out the instructions, helping individuals as necessary. You might have to provide additional explanations and prompts or ask further questions such as: *What is your number? Which number is three more than yours?* and so on.

Assessment opportunities

This activity should provide you with some indication of how well individual pupils understand the various sets and sequences. Watch how quickly they tackle each problem. It should be fairly easy to spot those who are wandering around, unsure of what to do.

Display ideas

Children could draw themselves with their number clearly displayed on the front, then cut these out and use them to form a display. These numbered paper pupils could be ordered or sequenced in various ways using instructions like those described above. Ask a different pupil or pair of pupils to do this each day using a particular set of instructions. You could also take photographs of various sets of pupils during the main activity and display these or use them as the basis for future activities and discussion.

Main activity

Organize the children to work in pairs or small groups, according to ability. Give each group a set of 1–100 number cards and one card from the activity pack. The activity card indicates the set or sequence they must make using their number cards. When the group have made their set or sequence they must record this on paper. They can then swap the activity card for another one. This can be organized in various ways. You could hold the pack of activity cards and distribute them according to the ability of the pupils in each group. Alternatively, you could produce two or three separate packs, graded and colour-coded according to ability. These could be placed somewhere in the classroom and pupils could help themselves from the appropriate pack.

Plenary

Use this time to present and praise the children's work. Also ask them to explain particular sets or sequences. Discuss a few examples from the activity pack, gradually increasing the level of difficulty.

Suggestion(s) for extension

Make sure you give able pupils the more challenging activity cards, for example 'groups of three numbers that add up to 25', or produce a separate pack for them to pick from as described above.

Suggestion(s) for support

Less able pupils can look for some of the more straightforward sets and sequences. You might also want these pupils to work with a smaller set of number cards, for example a set of 1–25 cards. These groups are also likely to need adult assistance during the main activity.

Assessment opportunities

Pupils' written work should provide useful evidence of their ability to identify various sets and sequences. However, it is also important to observe carefully when pupils are making the sets and sequences in groups. Sometimes one pupil does much of the work while others do little, even when the children have been grouped according to ability.

Reference to photocopiable sheet

Photocopiable page 119 provides a set of activity cards which the children use in conjunction with a set of 1–100 number cards. The activity cards are cut out and given to the children who must use their number cards to follow the set or sequence given on the card.

Sets and sequences	
The five smallest numbers	The five biggest numbers
Numbers less than 12	Numbers between 5 and 15
Numbers between 20 and 30	Numbers between 34 and 43
Odd numbers up to 21	Even numbers up to 20
Odd numbers between 35 and 45	Even numbers from 70 to 80
The five biggest odd numbers	The five biggest even numbers
Counting in 5s up to 25	Counting in 10s up to 100
Counting in 5s from 50 to 100	Counting in 3s up to 30
Counting in 4s up to 40	Pairs of numbers that add up to 10
Counting in 10s starting at 5	Counting in 10s starting at 3
Counting in 5s starting at 2. Stop at 52.	Counting in 4s starting at 1. Stop at 45.
Counting in 3s starting at 2. Stop at 50.	Groups of three numbers that add up to 25
Multiples of 6	Multiples of 7
Multiples of 8	Multiples of 9

Calculations and problem-solving

The boundary between knowing addition, subtraction, multiplication and division facts and being able to calculate mentally is a blurred one. Initially pupils will not be able to recall answers instantly; they will need to think and work things out in their heads. However, with reinforcement and practice, what were once the results of mental calculations will eventually become memorized facts. This section of the book, therefore, contains activities which focus on both number facts and mental calculations, as well as the early development of pencil and paper methods. Traditionally, there has been a heavy emphasis on the development, reinforcement and practise of standard pencil and paper routines at the expense of mental methods. However, it is important to ensure that mental methods are always seen as a first resort and therefore given appropriate emphasis. This is reflected in the balance of activities in this section.

You will see that the same learning objective is often repeated in several activities. This is because pupils need to develop their mental skills and their knowledge of number facts in a wide range of contexts. Children will soon grow tired of working through pages of 'sums' and so they need to be provided with alternatives which will motivate them to learn. The activities in this section therefore comprise games, puzzles, practical work, problem-solving and investigations.

DOMINO ADDITIONS

To develop knowledge of addition facts. To sort dominoes according to the sums of spots on each half.

†† *Whole-class introduction followed by work in small groups and a whole-class plenary.*

🕐 *Introduction 5–10 minutes; main activity 15–20 minutes; plenary 10–15 minutes; total 30–45 minutes.*

Previous skills/knowledge needed
Children will need to have some early experience of addition involving numbers up to 10.

Key background information
While children are developing their knowledge of addition facts it is important that they have access to practical apparatus or visual prompts. This enables them to make sense of what can otherwise be a very abstract concept. In the early stages children often use counters and cubes but in this activity the spots on dominoes provide the link between the concrete and the abstract. Some pupils will need to count the spots on each half separately and find the total by counting them all again. Others will be able to hold one number in their head and count on from there,

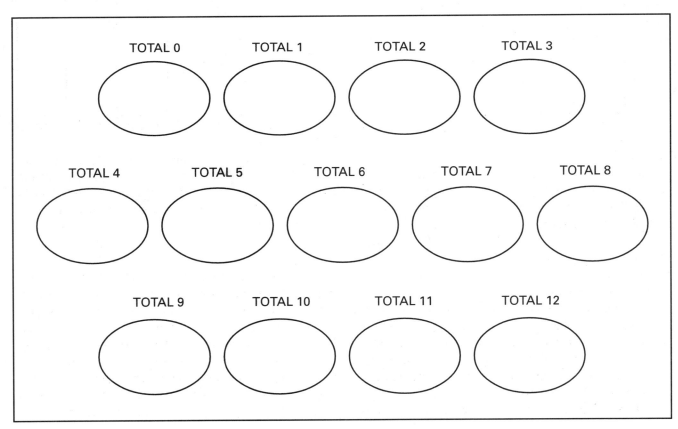

while some will be starting to remember the answers as facts that can be recalled instantly without any counting or calculation.

Preparation

Each group will need a large sheet of paper with thirteen rings or boxes drawn on it. The rings or boxes will need to be labelled 'Total 0', 'Total 1', 'Total 2', and so on up to 'Total 12', as shown on the opposite page. The rings or boxes do not have to be arranged or labelled in any particular order but they need to be large enough for the dominoes to fit inside them.

During the main activity pupils will be asked to sort the dominoes, placing them in the appropriate ring. Use photocopiable page 118 to make one set of paper or card dominoes. They could be made more durable by laminating them or covering them with clear sticky plastic sheet. These will be needed during the plenary. You will also need to draw on a large sheet of paper a copy of the diagram shown below. The columns will need to be at least as wide as the card dominoes.

of the halves and ask the children how many spots there are on it. Write the number on the board. Repeat this for the other half. Ask how many spots there are altogether and write this on the board. Ask children to explain how they worked out the answer (there may be several different strategies being used as described in 'Key background information'). Complete the board-work by writing a plus sign between the first two numbers and an equals sign before the total. Explain this notation to the pupils if they are not already familiar with it, introducing language such as 'add' and 'plus'. Hold up another domino and repeat the process.

Main activity

Organize the children into groups and give each group one set of dominoes and a large sheet of paper with labelled rings or boxes drawn on it. Tell them to spread out the dominoes, face down. Pupils should then take it in turns to pick a domino. They must then call out the addition sum that corresponds to their domino, for example 'Three plus four equals seven' and then place the domino in the

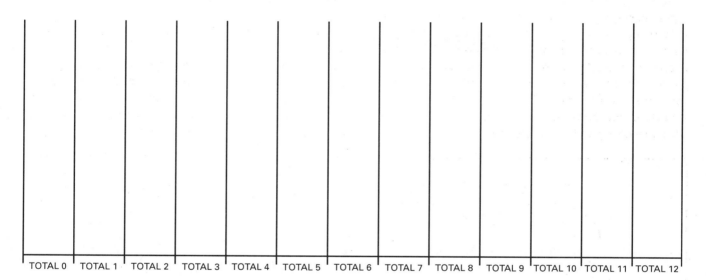

TOTAL 0	TOTAL 1	TOTAL 2	TOTAL 3	TOTAL 4	TOTAL 5	TOTAL 6	TOTAL 7	TOTAL 8	TOTAL 9	TOTAL 10	TOTAL 11	TOTAL 12

Resources

One set of paper or card dominoes (made using photocopiable page 118), large sheets of paper as described in 'Preparation', one set of dominoes per group, Blu-Tack, pencils, paper, board/flip chart.

What to do

Introduction

If the children have not used dominoes before then start by asking questions such as: *Does anyone know what dominoes look like? What numbers of spots do you see on a domino? Which domino will have the biggest number of spots? Which one will have the fewest spots?* and so on. Make sure pupils appreciate that a domino has two halves and that there are spots on each half.

Hold up one domino for the class to see. Point to one

appropriate ring or box. You might want each pupil to record their additions on their own sheet of paper using the appropriate symbols. The children take turns to pick a domino until all the dominoes have been placed on the large sheet of paper.

Plenary

Start by asking the children if they can remember which ring had the most dominoes in it and which had the fewest. Then spend the remaining time checking pupils' responses by sorting a set of dominoes in a slightly different way. Give out the set of paper or card dominoes you prepared earlier, one domino per pupil (some pupils might have to share). Explain to the children that they must come out, one at a time, and stick their domino in the appropriate column of the large diagram you prepared earlier.

When all 28 dominoes have been stuck onto the diagram, discuss it with the children. You could start by simply asking them what they notice about the shape that has been formed. They might describe it in terms of 'steps' or 'hill-shaped'. It might be appropriate at this stage to introduce the expression 'block-graph' or 'bar-chart'. Additional questions could include: *Which total do we get most often? Which totals do we get least often? Which totals do we get exactly three times?* and so on.

Suggestion(s) for extension

Ask pupils to pick two dominoes at a time and add up all four numbers, although they would not be able to sort them in the same way as with a single domino. Another possibility is to use commercially available sets of dominoes which go up to double-twelve. Alternatively, you could make a set yourself.

Suggestion(s) for support

During the main activity spend much of your time with the least able group providing appropriate prompts and asking further questions, for example: *How many spots are there on this half? How many spots on this half?* and *How many spots altogether?* At first these pupils need not be concerned with recording their work and instead should concentrate on developing their knowledge of addition facts.

Assessment opportunities

Working with a less able group will give you an insight into the children's knowledge and understanding of addition. Try to ascertain which pupils are finding the total by counting all of the spots again and which pupils are holding a number in their head and counting on. The children's written work will also provide valuable assessment evidence.

Opportunities for IT

The totals derived during the plenary can be summarized on a spreadsheet or other data-handling software and used to produce a bar chart. This could be compared with the block diagram produced using the dominoes themselves.

Display ideas

During this activity a set of dominoes is sorted in two ways: into labelled rings drawn on a large sheet of paper and into columns to form a block-graph. Stick paper or card dominoes onto the two diagrams and display them in the classroom.

Reference to photocopiable sheet

Photocopiable page 118 provides a set of dominoes. These should be photocopied onto card and then cut out for the children to use during the plenary session.

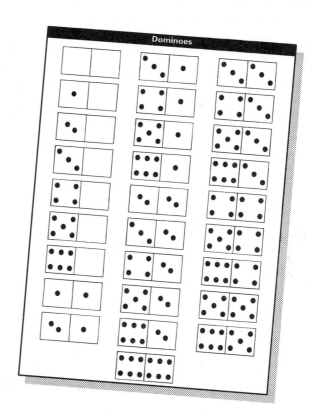

DOMINO DIFFERENCES

To understand the notion of 'difference'. To develop knowledge of subtraction facts. To sort dominoes according to the differences between spots on each half.

†† *Whole-class introduction followed by work in small groups and a whole-class plenary.*

⏲ *Introduction 5–10 minutes; main activity 15–20 minutes; plenary 10–15 minutes; total 30–45 minutes.*

Previous skills/knowledge needed

Children will need to have some early experience of subtraction involving numbers up to 10.

Key background information

This activity is similar to the previous activity 'Domino additions' but this time dominoes are used to reinforce subtraction facts.

Preparation

Each group will need a large sheet of paper with seven rings or boxes drawn on it. The rings or boxes will need to be labelled 'Difference 0', 'Difference 1', 'Difference 2', and so on up to 'Difference 6'. During the main activity pupils will sort the dominoes, placing them in the appropriate ring. Use photocopiable page 118 to make one set of paper or card dominoes. These are needed during the plenary. You will also need to draw on a large sheet of paper a copy of the diagram shown below. The columns will need to be at least as wide as the card dominoes.

Resources

One set of paper or card dominoes (made using photocopiable page 118), large sheets of paper as described above, one set of dominoes per group, various objects (such as cubes, counters, bean-bags), pencils, paper, board/flip chart.

What to do

Introduction

Ask two pupils to come out and stand at the front of the classroom. Give one pupil three objects (use the cubes, counters, bean-bags, and so on that you collected earlier) and the other pupil five objects (use the same type of object for both pupils). Try to develop the children's understanding of the concept of 'difference'. Start by asking how many objects each child has got and record the two numbers on the board. Ensure that the 5 is written to the left of the 3. Then ask how many more one pupil has got than the other and record the answer on the board. You might want to use language such as 'extras' or 'difference' and could demonstrate this by asking both pupils to place one object on the floor at the same time, then another object, then another object. One pupil will be left with nothing while the other is left with two extra objects. Finally, ask the children what sort of arithmetic they were doing to work out the difference. Complete the board-work by writing a subtraction sign between the first two numbers and an equals sign before the answer. Remind children of the language associated with subtraction, such as 'take away', 'minus' and 'subtract'. If necessary, repeat the activity with different amounts of objects.

If the pupils have not used dominoes before then introduce this resource by asking questions such as: *Does anyone know what dominoes look like? What numbers of spots do you see on a domino? Which domino will have the biggest number of spots? Which one will have the fewest spots?* and so on. Make sure pupils appreciate that a domino has two halves and that there are spots on each half. Hold up one domino (choose one that has a different amount on each half) and ask how many spots there are on each side. Record this on the board. Then ask how many more spots there are on one half than on the other, reinforcing the use of the word 'difference'. Record the answer on the board and complete the subtraction by writing in the appropriate symbols.

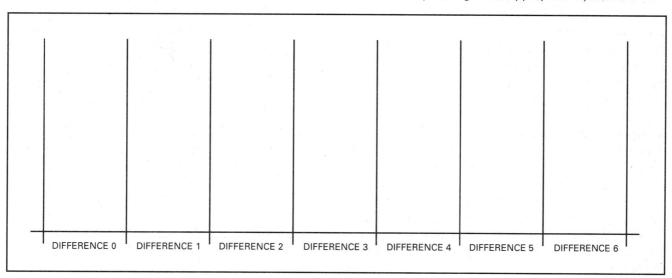

DIFFERENCE 0	DIFFERENCE 1	DIFFERENCE 2	DIFFERENCE 3	DIFFERENCE 4	DIFFERENCE 5	DIFFERENCE 6

Main activity

Organize the children into groups and give each group of pupils one set of dominoes and a large sheet of paper with labelled rings or boxes drawn on it. Also give each child a sheet of paper on which to record their subtractions. Tell them to spread out the dominoes, face down. Pupils should then take it in turns to pick a domino. They must then call out the subtraction which corresponds to their domino, for example 'six take-away four equals two' and place it in the appropriate ring or box. Each pupil could record their subtractions on their own piece of paper using the appropriate symbols. Children should take turns to pick a domino until all the dominoes have been placed on the large sheet of paper.

Plenary

Ask the children if they can remember which ring contained the most dominoes and which had the fewest. Then check their responses by carrying out the following whole-class activity. Give out the set of paper or card dominoes you prepared earlier, one domino per pupil (some pupils might have to share). Pupils must come out, one at a time, and stick their domino in the appropriate column of the large diagram you prepared earlier.

When the pupils have used up all of the dominoes, ask them to describe the shape that has been formed. It is likely that pupils will describe it in terms of 'steps'.

You could also use this as an opportunity to introduce pupils to the idea of a 'block-graph' or 'bar-chart'.

Suggestion(s) for extension

More able children could repeat the activity using sets of dominoes that go up to double-twelve (these are available commercially or you could make a set yourself).

Suggestion(s) for support

During the main activity spend much of your time with any groups of less able pupils, providing prompts and asking additional questions, for example: *How many spots are there on this half? How many spots on this half? Which half has the most spots? How many extra spots are there on this half?*

Assessment opportunities

If you work with a group of less able pupils observe them carefully and ask them to explain how they are working out the differences. There are a number of possibilities. Some pupils might count on from the lower number, some might 'remove' the lower number from the higher, and some might try to pair-off spots on each half to see how many are left over.

The other children's written work will provide valuable evidence of their ability to subtract single-digit numbers.

Opportunities for IT

The data obtained during the plenary could be summarized on a spreadsheet or other data-handling software and used to produce a bar chart. This could be compared with the block diagram produced using the dominoes themselves.

Display ideas

The children can stick a set of paper or card dominoes onto one of the large sheets of paper which have the labelled rings or boxes drawn on them. This can then be displayed on the wall alongside the block-graph produced during the plenary.

Reference to photocopiable sheet

Photocopiable page 118 provides a set of domino shapes which can be used to make your own sets of dominoes.

DOMINO SQUARES

To develop knowledge of addition facts. To apply this knowledge in a problem-solving situation.

†† *Whole-class introduction followed by individual work and a whole-class plenary.*

⏲ *Introduction 10–15 minutes; main activity 25–30 minutes; plenary 10–15 minutes; total 45–60 minutes.*

Previous skills/knowledge needed

Children should already have some experience of simple addition.

Key background information

It is important that children spend much time developing and practising their addition skills. However, they will soon grow tired of working through page after page of 'sums'. It is therefore important to provide a wide range of contexts within which the necessary skills can be used and applied. The activity described here is a problem-solving situation that requires more than just a knowledge of addition facts. Children will need to think carefully about what they are doing, make choices and decisions, and use trial and improvement methods.

Preparation

For the second part of the main activity children will need a copy of either photocopiable page 120 or 121. Some pupils might use both sheets so ensure there are sufficient spare copies. You will also need several sets of dominoes, If you do not have sufficient sets you can make some extra ones by copying photocopiable page 118 onto thin card. (If you have carried out the previous two activities you may already have these.) Depending on how far the children get with the extension activity, you may need to make up some worksheets of your own for children to complete (see 'Suggestion(s) for extension' on page 66).

Resources

Sets of dominoes (several pupils can share a set but the more sets the better), photocopiable pages 120 and 121, photocopiable page 118 (optional), paper, pencils, board/flip chart.

What to do

Introduction

If children have not used dominoes before then first ensure that they are familiar with them. Ask questions such as: *What does a domino look like? What numbers of spots do you see on a domino? Which domino has the biggest number of spots? Which one has the fewest spots?* and so on. The key points to stress are that each domino has two halves and there are spots on each half.

Pick two dominoes and hold them up together to form a square. You can hold them either vertically side-by-side, or horizontally one above the other. Draw the dominoes on the board or alternatively prepare large drawings of them in advance. The drawing should look something like this.

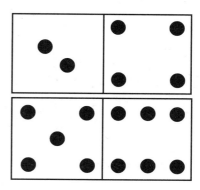

Point to the two top numbers and ask the children to tell you the total or the sum (use language which they are accustomed to). You might want to use the expression 'top row'. Write the total to the right of the top row. Repeat this for the bottom row, again writing the total to the right of the domino. Then ask children to tell you the total for the left-hand column. Point the numbers out and use appropriate terminology to explain the question. Write the total below the left column. Repeat this for the right-hand column. The example shown above would look like this when complete.

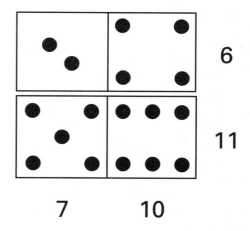

Repeat the whole process if you feel it is necessary.

Main activity

Organize the children into pairs and give each pair some paper and a set of dominoes to share but stress that the children should work individually. Each pupil should pick any two dominoes, place them side by side, record the dominoes on their sheet of paper (they could use either spots or numbers) and finally work out the row and column totals.

When you feel that individual pupils have had sufficient

practice at this activity, and understand the idea of row and column totals, give them a copy of either photocopiable page 120 or 121 (it does not matter which – the sheets are not differentiated). Explain to them that they must fit two dominoes into each square so that the row and column totals shown on the sheet are correct. They must then draw the two dominoes in the square before moving on to the next one.

Plenary

Start by asking the children to explain the strategies they were using when attempting photocopiable pages 120 and 121. Copy a square from one of the photocopiable sheets onto the board so that pupils can refer to it when explaining their methods.

Next, draw the problem shown below on the board and ask the class to work out the solution. Record the solution on the board. Then ask pupils to see if there is another solution. See how many different solutions there are to this problem and record each one on the board.

Suggestion(s) for extension

During the first part of the main activity, ask able pupils to arrange two dominoes to form a square so that all the row and column totals are the same. It is in fact not possible to do this but see whether the children can work this out for themselves and give an explanation why. (The numbers in diagonally opposite corners would have to be equal and this can only be achieved by using two identical dominoes.)

Altogether, there are fourteen squares to be filled on photocopiable pages 120 and 121. They require a complete set of 28 dominoes. Using one set of dominoes, it is possible to arrange them over the two sheets so that all of the row and column totals are correct. Each domino can only be used once. Able children could be given a copy of both sheets and attempt to do this.

You could make up challenging worksheets of your own similar to photocopiable pages 120 and 121. Use rectangles that will accommodate three dominoes such as the one shown below.

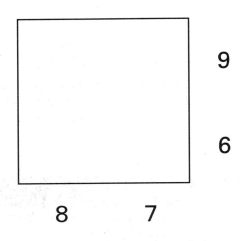
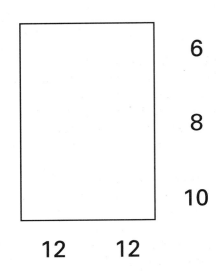

There are in fact eight solutions as shown below.

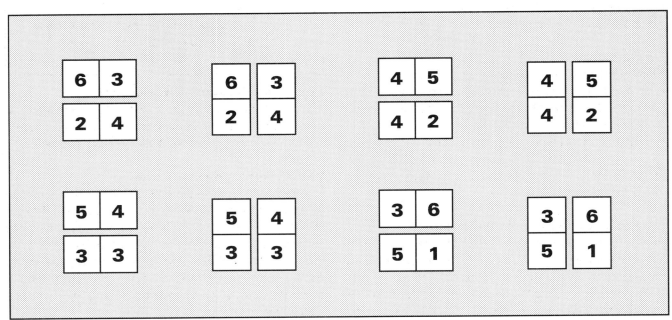

Suggestion(s) for support

The first part of the main activity should be accessible to less able children, although they might need some extra help at first until they have grasped the idea of row and column totals. Only let them move onto the second part of the main activity when you think they are ready for it.

Assessment opportunities

The work recorded on paper will provide evidence of the children's knowledge of addition facts. Observe pupils carefully during the second part of the main activity to ascertain the strategies they are using when completing the photocopiable sheets and also ask them to explain their methods to you. This will provide an insight into the way they think and their ability to solve problems.

Display ideas

Many of the solutions produced during this activity can be organized to form an interesting display. For example, one part of the display could show all of the possible solutions to a particular problem. For example, the problem discussed in the plenary had eight different solutions. Children could try to find a question which has even more solutions and use this as the basis of an on-going interactive display.

Reference to photocopiable sheets

Photocopiable page 118 can be used to make your own sets of dominoes. Copy each set onto a different coloured piece of card to avoid the sets getting mixed up.

Photocopiable pages 120 and 121 show squares which must be filled with two dominoes. Each of the domino squares on photocopiable sheets 120 and 121 can be solved in more than one way. The solutions above show how one complete set of dominoes can be used to cover both sheets.

THREE IN A ROW

To practise addition and subtraction facts in the context of a strategy game.

†† *Whole-class introduction followed by work in pairs and a whole-class plenary.*

⏱ *Introduction 5–10 minutes; main activity 20–25 minutes; plenary 5–10 minutes; total 30–45 minutes.*

Previous skills/knowledge needed

This activity provides an opportunity to practise skills that have already been taught and so it is assumed children will have some experience of addition and subtraction.

Key background information

Children must practise their mental skills and knowledge of number facts throughout Key Stages One and Two but this needs to be done in a wide range of contexts since children will soon become bored of doing the same sorts of activity over and over again. In this activity pupils play a strategy game but the main focus is on developing number skills. The activity can be adapted in many ways to suit a wide range of abilities.

Preparation

Prepare copies of photocopiable page 122 so that there is one for each pair of pupils. (It could be copied onto card or possibly laminated to make it more durable. It might be worth doing this because the same number grid can be used for several different activities during Key Stage One, for example the activity 'Find...' on page 73.) You might also like to prepare a few similar sheets of your own as described in the 'Suggestion(s) for extension' below. Each pair will also need a pack of twenty or thirty cards containing numbers in the range 1–10. Use photocopiable page 103 to produce these if necessary. Make one copy of the sheet, change the zero to a ten, and then photocopy it onto coloured card. Use a different colour for each pack so that children sitting close to one another do not get the cards mixed up. An alternative to using a pack of cards is to use a ten-sided dice. These are usually numbered 0–9 and so you will need to change the zero to a ten.

Resources

Photocopiable page 122, packs of 1–10 cards (or ten-sided dice), a supply of counters in two colours, calculators for checking, paper, pencils, board/flip chart.

What to do

Introduction

Start by spending a few minutes practising number facts and mental skills together. One possible way of doing this is to hold up a piece of card with a number on it (or write the number on the board) and tell the children that this is an answer. They must provide the question. This approach is self-differentiating since children will use only those operations they are comfortable with and select a level of complexity suitable for their own ability. You might like to impose additional constraints, for example you might tell a particular child to use subtraction or multiplication. This will allow you to challenge individual pupils or make them focus on areas of weakness.

Next, hold up two numbers in the range 1–10 (or write them on the board) and ask children to make answers with them. The obvious choices are addition and subtraction but you might have one or two able pupils who are able to multiply the two numbers. You could record each piece of arithmetic on the board. Repeat this for other pairs of numbers.

Main activity

Set the pupils to work in pairs using one copy of photocopiable page 122, a pack of cards in the range 1–10 (or a ten-sided dice) and a supply of counters in two colours. Each child will also need some paper on which to record their work. The first pupil in each pair should pick two cards from the pack (or roll the dice twice) and then either add or subtract the numbers to produce an answer. The child must then look for the answer on the photocopiable sheet and on finding it cover it with a counter of his or her colour (as the game progresses it might occasionally be impossible to place a counter on the grid because the appropriate answer is covered already). The children must clearly state to their opponent how they have obtained the answer and also record the arithmetic on paper (any disputes can be settled by checking with the calculator). If the arithmetic is incorrect then the counter cannot be placed on the sheet. Children must take it in turns to have a go. The objective is to get three counters next to each other in a line either horizontally, vertically or diagonally.

Plenary

Use the plenary for further whole-class oral practice of mental skills and recall of number facts. You may like to repeat the activities used in the introduction but this time use bigger numbers.

Suggestion(s) for extension

The basic activity described above can be adapted in many ways to make it more challenging. For example, children could use a pack of cards with numbers in the range 1–20; they could use a twelve or twenty-sided dice; they could pick three

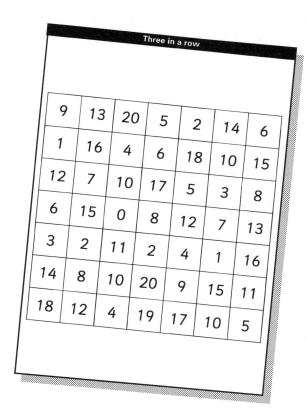

cards instead of just two, and so on. In all cases you will have to provide an alternative to photocopiable page 122, for example if pupils are rolling a twenty-sided dice then they will need a grid containing numbers up to 40 (and possibly higher if they are using multiplication).

Suggestion(s) for support

Less able children could focus solely on addition at first if you think this is appropriate. You might also want to remove the strategy element so that pupils can concentrate on the number skills, that is, their objective could be simply to get as many counters of their own colour on the grid as possible rather than be concerned with getting three in a row.

Assessment opportunities

During the introduction and plenary, match your questions carefully to the abilities of individual pupils so that they are being challenged in their areas of weakness. Make a mental note of how individual pupils respond to this. During the main activity, try to spend some of your time working with a group of less able pupils. Observe their progress carefully and judge when they are ready to move on to using subtraction.

Reference to photocopiable sheet

Photocopiable page 122 displays a number grid. Using a pack of cards, children use various number strategies to find the numbers on the grid and then cover them with counters.

ADDITION WITH HTU CARDS

To consolidate understanding of place value. To develop and practise both mental and pencil and paper methods for addition.

†† *Whole-class introduction followed by individual work and a whole-class plenary.*

🕐 *Introduction 10–15 minutes; main activity 25–30 minutes; plenary 10–15 minutes; total 45–60 minutes.*

Previous skills/knowledge needed

It is assumed that children will have some experience of addition involving two-digit numbers and are familiar with numbers beyond 100.

Key background information

Mental agility with numbers requires an understanding of place value and so it is important that children are constantly reminded of the underlying structure of our number system. This activity requires pupils to break numbers into their constituent parts before adding them, thus reinforcing place value. Initially the focus is on mental skills but pencil and paper methods can be developed naturally from these. For example, the traditional pencil and paper method for adding 284 and 469 would involve 'carrying' but here is an alternative approach.

	284
	469
Add the hundreds (say *200 plus 400*) to get	**600**
Add the tens (say *80 plus 60*) to get	**140**
Add the units to get	**13**
Add (mentally) to get	**753**

This approach is based on a sound understanding of place value and it follows on naturally from mental methods. It also encourages and reinforces both place value and mental agility. There is no reason at all why children should not be encouraged to use methods such as these and they do offer benefits in terms of developing understanding.

Preparation

Ideally each pupil should have their own set of HTU cards although it is possible for pupils to share a set and some pupils may not need to use them at all. Photocopiable pages 97–100 need to be photocopied onto card and then cut up to make the sets of HTU cards. There will be eighteen cards in a set if the pupils are to make two-digit numbers and twenty-seven if they are to make three-digit numbers. You will also need to write a set of addition problems for the children to solve (see the main activity on the next page).

Resources

Sets of HTU cards (made using photocopiable pages 97–100), paper, pencils, board/flip chart.

What to do

Introduction

Ask a child to give you an example of a two-digit number. Write the number the child suggests on the board. Point to the tens digit and ask the class what it represents. Similarly point to the units digit and ask what this represents. Quickly make the number with your HTU cards (or ask a pupil to make it) and demonstrate what each digit represents. Write the constituent parts on the board to the right of the original number so that it looks something like this.

$$35 = 30 + 5$$

Repeat this with another two-digit number, writing it underneath the first one and again ask pupils to explain what each digit represents. Demonstrate using the HTU cards if necessary. Complete the board work so that it looks something like this.

$$35 = 30 + 5$$

$$48 = 40 + 8$$

Now ask the children to add the two original numbers and explain the method they used. Hopefully these will be based on the information written on the board (add 30 and 40 and then add 5 and 8). Explain and reinforce this approach.

Ask children to provide two new two-digit numbers and write them side-by-side on the board like this.

$$67 \quad 24$$

Again, point to a digit and ask the children what it represents. Make both numbers with the HTU cards and use these to reinforce understanding if necessary. Now write a plus sign between the two numbers and ask the children to first of all add the tens digits. Hold up the tens cards from each number so that the pupils are clear what it is they are adding. (Remember to refer to them as 60 and 20, not 6 and 2.) Then ask the children to add the units digits, again holding up the units cards from the two numbers. Extend the board work so that it looks like this.

$$67 + 24 = 80 + 11$$

Finally ask the children to work out the final answer and record it on the board like this.

$$67 + 24 = 80 + 11 = 91$$

Repeat this process if necessary using two new two-digit numbers.

Main activity

Hand out some paper and the HTU cards and ask the children to complete various additions (for instance 35 + 24 =) using the HTU cards as an aid. The problems you wish to set the children can be written on the board or presented as a worksheet. Ensure that the additions are matched to the abilities of the pupils and follow sensible

lines of progression. Children must first make the two numbers with the HTU cards. They must then add the tens, then add the units and finally add the two answers together. Pupils can record their work as shown in the example above.

Plenary

Work through one or two further examples in the same way as you did during the introduction but this time use three-digit numbers, for example:

$$154 + 318 = 400 + 60 + 12 = 472$$

Use the HTU cards to ensure that the children understand what each digit represents and to explain how the hundreds are combined, followed by the tens and finally the units. Remember to say, for example, '100 plus 300' rather than '1 plus 3'.

Suggestion(s) for extension

Provide questions that are matched to the ability of the individual pupils. Some pupils will be capable of quickly moving on to additions involving three-digit numbers. Some children will not need to use the HTU cards although they should still record their work in the way that has been indicated.

Suggestion(s) for support

Give less able pupils straightforward additions to start with, and encourage them to use the HTU cards throughout. They will also require additional support.

Assessment opportunities

The children's responses during the introduction and plenary will indicate their understanding of place value. During the main activity, ask individual pupils additional questions to gain further insights. The children's written work should allow you to identify any problems and weaknesses.

Display ideas

Use the HTU cards to make a display that reminds children of the constituent parts of various two and three-digit numbers and also shows how these numbers can be added.

Reference to photocopiable sheets

If pupils are going to be making three-digit numbers then you will need to use photocopiable pages 97–100. If only two-digit numbers are to be made then you will need only the first two sheets. The triangle at the right-hand side of each card is there to help you align the cards. Hold the units card, the tens card and the hundreds card so that the triangles are aligned and held in place between your thumb and fingers.

ARITHMETIC SEARCH

To develop knowledge of addition and subtraction facts.

†† *Whole-class introduction followed by individual work and whole-class plenary.*

⏱ *Introduction 5–10 minutes; main activity 20–25 minutes; plenary 5–10 minutes; total 30–45 minutes.*

Previous skills/knowledge needed

Children will need to have some knowledge of addition and subtraction facts.

Key background information

This activity provides pupils with another opportunity to develop and consolidate their knowledge of number facts. Much time needs to be spent on this during Key Stage One but in order to maintain high levels of pupil interest it is important to make use of as many different contexts as possible.

Preparation

Make copies of photocopiable page 123, one per pupil. Also make an enlarged copy to use as a visual aid during the introduction and plenary. For the extension activity prepare a worksheet with the arithmetic signs missing.

Resources

Photocopiable page 123, pencils, squared paper, paper, board/flip chart. For the extension activity – a prepared sheet with the arithmetic signs missing.

What to do

Introduction

Spend the first few minutes practising mental skills and knowledge of number facts. You could hold up a piece of card with a number on it (or write the number on the board) and tell pupils that this is an answer. They must provide the question. Ask several different pupils of varying ability to provide a question. You could impose constraints on individual pupils so as to challenge them or to focus on areas of weakness, for example: *You mustn't use addition* or *You must use a two-figure number*. Repeat this process with a different number.

Next write the numbers 3, 9 and 12 on the board with spaces between them as shown below.

3   9   12

Explain to the children that this is a piece of arithmetic but the signs have been missed out. Ask them which signs are missing and where they should go.

Repeat this with other examples such as:

15	**8**	**7**		(15 − 8 = 7 or 15 = 8 + 7)
6	**5**	**2**	**9**	(6 + 5 − 2 = 9 or 6 + 5 = 2 + 9)
4	**9**	**5**		(4 = 9 − 5 but **not** 4 − 9 = 5)

Hold up an enlarged copy of photocopiable page 123 and explain to the children that it contains lots of pieces of arithmetic (you might need to stress that all of the necessary signs have been included). Ask pupils if they can spot one of the pieces of arithmetic and point it out to the rest of the class. See if anyone can spot one which reads downwards. Ensure that all pupils realize that the arithmetic can be read across or down but not diagonally.

Main activity

Give each child a copy of photocopiable page 123 and ask them to work individually to find as many pieces of arithmetic as possible. They should then record these at the bottom of the sheet or on a separate piece of paper.

Those children who complete the initial task can go on to produce an arithmetic search of their own on squared paper and pass it on to another pupil to use.

Plenary

Look at the pieces of arithmetic the children have found on the sheet. These can be recorded on the board and children can check them off against their own lists.

Suggestion(s) for extension

The follow-up activity described above should provide a challenge for many pupils. Another extension, suitable for all pupils rather than just the more able, is a worksheet on the theme of missing signs as covered in the introduction. If you have prepared such a sheet, pass this to the children for them to complete.

Suggestion(s) for support

There are plenty of fairly straightforward pieces of arithmetic on the sheet which all the children should be capable of finding. However, if some children are struggling you could provide them with a list of the arithmetic that can be found on the sheet and ask them to find it. In this case the focus of the activity will be on pairing or matching skills. Another alternative is to provide clues, for example you could tell them the numbers used in each piece of arithmetic but not the signs.

Assessment opportunities

During the main activity watch out for any obvious errors in the children's recording of the arithmetic and ask further questions as necessary. In particular, focus on those children whose knowledge of number facts you know to be weak.

Display ideas

The arithmetic search sheets devised by the pupils during the second part of the main activity would form a valuable display. Encourage children to keep trying to find the arithmetic on these sheets and build up an on-going list as part of the display.

Reference to photocopiable sheet

Photocopiable page 123 provides a number grid showing various pieces of arithmetic. The children must try to find as many pieces as possible on the sheet.

The following arithmetic can be found on the sheet.

Reading horizontally left to right:

$$2 + 5 = 7$$
$$3 + 3 = 6$$
$$8 - 3 = 5$$
$$5 + 4 = 9$$
$$4 + 6 = 10$$
$$3 = 2 + 1$$
$$2 + 1 + 5 = 8$$
$$11 = 5 + 4 + 1 + 1$$
$$9 - 5 = 4$$
$$4 + 3 + 3 = 10$$
$$6 = 8 - 2$$
$$7 = 2 + 5$$
$$2 + 5 + 5 = 12$$

Reading vertically downwards:

$$5 - 4 = 1$$
$$7 = 6 + 1$$
$$9 + 1 = 10$$
$$8 + 3 = 11$$
$$3 + 2 = 5$$
$$5 = 1 + 4$$
$$4 + 5 + 1 = 10$$
$$9 = 8 + 1$$
$$7 = 3 + 4$$
$$2 = 5 - 3$$
$$8 + 1 + 3 = 12$$
$$1 = 0 + 1$$
$$3 + 5 = 8$$
$$10 - 4 = 6$$
$$11 - 4 = 7$$
$$5 - 3 = 2$$

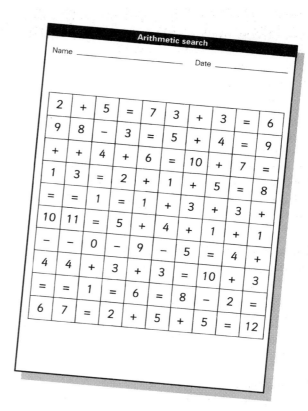

Arithmetic search

2	+	5	=	7	3	+	3	=	6
9	8	–	3	=	5	+	4	=	9
+	+	4	+	6	=	10	+	7	=
1	3	=	2	+	1	+	5	=	8
=	=	1	=	1	+	3	+	3	+
10	11	=	5	+	4	+	1	+	1
–	–	0	–	9	–	5	=	4	+
4	4	+	3	+	3	=	10	+	3
=	=	1	=	6	=	8	–	2	=
6	7	=	2	+	5	+	5	=	12

FIND...

To develop knowledge of addition facts involving numbers up to 20. To practise mental arithmetic skills.

†† *Whole-class introduction followed by individual work and whole-class plenary.*

🕐 *Introduction 5–10 minutes; main activity 30–35 minutes; plenary 10–15 minutes; total 45–60 minutes.*

Previous skills/knowledge needed

Children should have some experience of addition and subtraction of numbers up to 20.

Key background information

This open-ended activity provides children with an opportunity to consolidate and practise important number skills that have been introduced on an earlier occasion. It requires pupils to use a grid containing numbers up to 20 to find pairs or groups of numbers that satisfy particular conditions based on addition and subtraction. It is possible to adapt the activity to suit pupils of all abilities.

Preparation

Make copies of photocopiable pages 122 and 124 so that there is one of each sheet per pupil. Also write a random selection of numbers in the range 1–20 on the board or on a large sheet of paper. You will need to refer to these during the introduction. You may like to use photocopiable page 125 for those children carrying out the support activity. For the extension activity you may wish to create a number grid which includes numbers beyond 20.

Resources
Copies of photocopiable pages 122 and 124, paper, pencils, board/flip chart/large sheet of paper. For the support activity – photocopiable page 125 (optional). For the extension activity – a number grid with numbers beyond 20 (optional).

What to do
Introduction
Ensure that all the children can see the numbers you have written on the board or on the sheet of paper and use these as the basis for some whole-class quick-fire practice of mental calculation skills and knowledge of number facts. Ask questions such as: *Which two numbers add up to 20? Which two have a difference of 5? Which one is five less than 12? Tell me three numbers on the board whose total is 30* and so on. Carefully match the questions to the abilities of individual pupils and use this as an opportunity to revise and perhaps introduce the wide range of mathematical language associated with addition and subtraction. When children give you an answer, ask them how it would be written using numbers and symbols. Record the arithmetic on the board for everyone to see.

Main activity
Tell the children that they are now going to work individually using one copy each of photocopiable pages 122 and 124. Hand these out and explain that they must look at the number grid on page 122 and find the pairs or sets of numbers specified on page 124. When they have found the numbers they must record them on paper. This could be in the form of arithmetic using numbers and symbols, for example 8 + 12 = 20, or it could be in the form of a drawing which indicates the numbers and their orientation on the grid. For example:

8
12

(Explain to the children that the lines of numbers they find on the grid can be horizontal or vertical. Also explain what is meant by 'four numbers that form a square' in the final question.) If anyone completes photocopiable page 124, then ask them to work through it again and find a second solution to each question.

Plenary
Work through some or all of the answers. Bear in mind that in almost every case the total can be made in more than one way (sometimes as many as six different ways). Also ask children to explain how they went about finding the totals.

Suggestion(s) for extension
Photocopiable page 124 provides examples of the sorts of targets you could set. Make up other more challenging worksheets based on the same number grid or on other grids which you have easy access to. Alternatively, make a grid of your own which includes numbers beyond 20. Children could also set targets of their own based on the original grid and pass these on to other pupils to find.

Suggestion(s) for support
It should be possible for less able children to answer the early instructions on photocopiable page 124, for example finding two numbers that add up to 5 and 10. If you feel that this is their limit then ask them to answer these two questions in as many ways as possible (there are two ways of making 5 and six ways of making 10).

If you feel that many of the questions are too demanding for some pupils then make a list of easier targets based on the original grid or perhaps based on a new grid containing lower numbers. For example the grid shown on photocopiable page 125 contains numbers up to 12 and so could be used in this way.

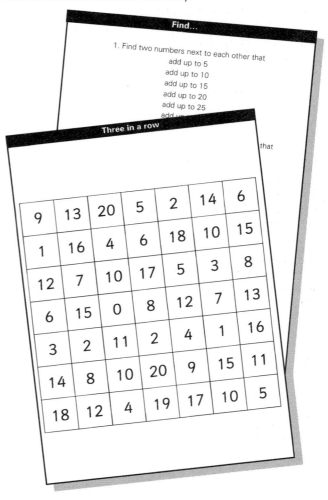

Assessment opportunities

The work recorded on photocopiable page 124 will indicate the children's knowledge of addition facts and their ability to add numbers mentally. Observe how they tackle the main activity and ask them to explain what they are doing. This will provide an insight into the way they work with number as well as their ability to use and apply mathematics.

Display ideas

Display an enlarged copy of the original grid on the wall together with the children's solutions to the questions. This could form the basis of an on-going attempt to find all the different ways of answering each problem. Children could add new solutions to the display as they find them.

Reference to photocopiable sheets

Photocopiable page 122 displays a number grid. Using this children must attempt to solve the problems on photocopiable page 124. The solution to the sheet is as follows:

Two numbers that add up to 5

| 3 | 2 | | 4 | 1 |

Two numbers that add up to 10

| 8 | 3 | 10 | 2 | 9 | 4 | 6 |
| 2 | 7 | 0 | 8 | 1 | | |

Two numbers that add up to 15

| 15 | 0 | | 10 | 5 |

Two numbers that add up to 20

| 2 | 8 | 14 | 6 | 8 | 12 | 16 | 4 | 7 | 13 |
| 18 | 12 |

Two numbers that add up to 25

| 17 | 15 | 20 | 5 | 10 | 15 |
| 8 | 10 |

Two numbers that add up to 30

| 18 | 12 | | 10 | 20 |

Three numbers that add up to 15

| 2 | 11 | 2 |

Three numbers that add up to 20

| 10 |
| 3 | | 0 | 8 | 12 |
| 7 |

Three numbers that add up to 25

2	15	12	11	17	5	3
18	2	4	10
5	8	9	4

Three numbers that add up to 30

8	4
2	9
20	17

Three numbers that add up to 35

18	3	9	15	11	12	4	19
5	14
12	18

Three numbers that add up to 40

| 13 |
| 16 | 4 | 19 | 17 |
| 11 |

Four in a line that add up to 25

4	0
10	11
0	10
11	4

Four in a line that add up to 30

| 5 |
| 12 |
| 4 |
| 9 |

Four in a line that add up to 35

| 10 | 17 | 5 | 3 | 15 | 0 | 8 | 12 |

Four in a line that add up to 40

| 16 |
| 7 | 8 | 12 | 7 | 13 |
| 15 |
| 2 |

Four in a line that add up to 45

13
16
11
5

Four in a line that add up to 50

4	19	17	10

Four in a line that add up to 55

20	9	15	11

Four in a square that add up to 35

2	4
20	9

20	5
4	6

Four in a square that add up to 40

12	7
6	15

Four in a square that add up to 45

14	6
10	15

Four in a square that add up to 65

20	9
19	17

DOUBLING BINGO

To practise mental doubling strategies involving numbers up to 10.

†† *Whole-class activity.*

🕐 *Introduction 5–10 minutes; main activity 15–20 minutes; plenary 10–15 minutes; total 30–45 minutes.*

Previous skills/knowledge needed
Children should have some experience of mental strategies for doubling numbers up to 10.

Key background information
Most children are introduced to the idea of doubling during Key Stage One but this, like all mental strategies, needs to be reinforced and practised regularly in a variety of contexts such as the game described here.

Preparation
For the main activity each child will need a 4 × 3 grid containing the numbers 1–12. Children could quickly draw such a grid themselves on squared paper at the start of the activity. Alternatively, draw this yourself and make copies for the whole class. For the support activity you may wish to provide the children with a prompt sheet of numbers (see 'Suggestion(s) for support' opposite).

Resources
Number grids (see 'Preparation'), one six-sided dice, squared paper, pencils. For the support activity – a prompt sheet (optional).

What to do
Introduction
Recap the previous work on doubles by asking questions such as: *Who can remember what a double is?* and *If I double a number, what do I do to it?* Follow this with some quick-fire mental practice involving doubles. Call out a number (or hold up a numbered card) and ask the children to double it. Occasionally stop and ask pupils to explain how they did the mental calculation.

Main activity
If you have not prepared a numbered grid in advance, show pupils how to produce a 4 × 3 grid containing the numbers 1–12 by demonstrating on the board or holding up an enlarged example. Alternatively, give them a copy of the grid you have produced.

Explain how to play doubling bingo. Tell the children that you will roll a six-sided dice and they can either cross off the number itself or its double. Stress that they can only do one or the other, not both. The winner is the first child to cross off all of his or her numbers. Start to play the game by rolling the dice and allowing pupils a short

period of time to cross a number off their grid. After several rolls of the dice pause to check on progress by asking: *Who has crossed off five numbers altogether, … six numbers altogether* and so on. Hopefully, one of the pupils will point out at some stage that it is impossible to win, although you might need to provide a few hints or ask pointed questions such as: *Is anyone close to winning? Which numbers have you not crossed off?* and *How long is it since you crossed off a number?*

Once it has been established that it is impossible to win the game, discuss the numbers that can and cannot be crossed off the grid (7, 9 and 11) and why. Then tell pupils that they can play the game again but this time they can decide which numbers appear on their grid. They must draw another 4 × 3 grid and write in 12 numbers of their own choice. Stress that numbers can be used more than once if they wish (for instance a pupil might want to include two 4s on their grid). Play the game again, reminding pupils of the rules, particularly that they can only cross off one number at a time.

When the game has been won, ask the winner to explain which numbers he or she included on the grid and why. Discuss the choices and reasons with the whole class.

Plenary

Discuss variations on the game, for example suppose a ten-sided dice was used. Ask the children which numbers they would include on their number grids. What would be the smallest and the biggest numbers? Which numbers would they not include? What about a twelve-sided dice? Again, which numbers would pupils include on their grids

and which ones would they avoid? What about a twenty-sided dice?

Suggestion(s) for extension

The open-ended nature of the main activity means that it is self-differentiating and therefore the more able pupils will be able to work at their own level when deciding which numbers to include on the grid. Some of the variations discussed in the plenary could form the basis of follow-up investigations for groups of able pupils.

Suggestion(s) for support

The nature of the activity is such that it should be accessible to less able pupils. Those who find it very difficult to work out doubles would benefit from adult assistance or perhaps you could provide them with a prompt sheet showing a list of numbers up to six with doubles written at the side.

Assessment opportunities

This activity produces little tangible assessment evidence but by listening carefully to the children's responses during the discussions you will learn much about their understanding of doubles and their ability to apply it.

Display ideas

Write brief instructions for the game on a piece of paper and display it on the wall. You could also display various filled in 'bingo cards' (for instance 4 × 3 grids) under two headings, 'You could win with these bingo cards' and 'You cannot win with these bingo cards – can you work out why?'.

DOUBLING THREE-IN-A-ROW

To practise mental doubling strategies involving single-digit numbers.

†† *Whole-class introduction followed by work in pairs and whole-class plenary.*

🕐 *Introduction 5–10 minutes; main activity 15–20 minutes; plenary 10–15 minutes; total 30–45 minutes.*

Previous skills/knowledge needed

Children should have some knowledge of doubles and doubling strategies.

Key background information

This activity provides another opportunity for children to develop their knowledge and understanding of doubles and to practise mental strategies for doubling.

Preparation

Prepare copies of photocopiable page 125, one for each pair of pupils. (You may like to copy it onto card or possibly laminate it to make it more durable. This is a worthwhile investment of time and money because these sorts of number grids can be used in many different ways.) You will also need to prepare some appropriate number grids for the extension activity.

Resources

Photocopiable page 125, six-sided dice, a supply of counters in two colours, calculators, paper, pencils (each pair will need one each of these items), board/flip chart. For the extension activity – appropriately adapted number grids.

What to do

Introduction

Spend a few minutes recapping earlier work on doubles by asking questions such as: *Who can tell me what a double is?* and *How do we double a number?* Follow this with some quick-fire mental practice involving doubles. Call out a number (or hold up a numbered card) and ask the children to double it. Occasionally, stop and ask children to explain how they did the mental calculation. You might want to explore the relationship between doubles and even numbers. Write several doubles on the board (use some of the answers to your quick-fire questions) and ask the children what they notice about them all or what type of numbers they are.

Main activity

Organize the children into pairs and give each pair a copy of photocopiable page 125, a six-sided dice, a supply of counters in two colours, a calculator and some paper. To play, the first pupil should roll the dice and then cover either the number itself or its double on the grid with a counter of his or her colour. Stress to the children that they can do one or the other but not both. Only one number is covered at a time (although as the game progresses it might occasionally be impossible to place a counter on the grid because the appropriate number is covered already). Children must state clearly to their opponent how they have obtained the number, for example by saying 'double 4 is 8'. You might also want the children to record their doubles on paper. Any disputes can be settled by checking with the calculator. If the double has not been worked out correctly then the counter is not placed on the sheet. Tell the children to take it in turns to have a go and explain that the objective is for each child to get three counters of his

or her own colour next to each other in a line either horizontally, vertically or diagonally.

Plenary

Tell the children that there is one number on the grid that is impossible to cover and ask them to work out which one it is (7, in the centre of the grid). Encourage pupils to explain their answers and to provide you with other examples of numbers that would be impossible to cover. Also discuss which numbers could and could not be covered if other dice had been used, for example ten, twelve and twenty-sided dice.

Suggestion(s) for extension

Children can play the game using a ten, twelve or twenty-sided dice in conjunction with an appropriate number grid. You will need to work out which numbers must be included on the grid (notice that 9 and 11 do not appear on the original grid) and prepare copies beforehand.

Suggestion(s) for support

You might want to remove the strategy element so that pupils can concentrate on the doubling skills, that is, their objective could be simply to get as many counters of their own colour on the grid as possible rather than be concerned with getting three in a row.

Assessment opportunities

During the introduction, match your quick-fire questions to the abilities of the children and make a mental note of how individuals respond. If you spend some of your time during the main activity working with a group of less able pupils observe how well they recall and work out doubles.

Reference to photocopiable sheet

Photocopiable page 125 provides a number grid. Using a dice, the children attempt to place counters over the numbers on the grid.

Doubling three-in-a-row						
1	10	6	5	2	3	6
4	8	2	4	10	8	4
2	3	12	6	1	2	10
6	1	5	7	3	6	4
2	4	10	2	8	5	12
6	12	8	6	4	1	2
5	4	3	12	2	6	4

MULTIPLICATION PRACTICE

To develop knowledge of multiplication facts involving 2s, 5s and 10s.

†† *Whole-class introduction followed by work in pairs and a whole-class plenary.*

🕐 *Introduction 10–15 minutes; main activity 25–30 minutes; plenary 10–15 minutes; total 45–60 minutes.*

Previous skills/knowledge needed

It is assumed that children will have started to use multiplication facts involving 2s, 5s and 10s.

Key background information

Sound mental and pencil and paper arithmetic skills depend on children being able to recall multiplication facts speedily but this can only be achieved with constant reinforcement and practice. This activity focuses on multiples of 2, 5 and 10, and provides just one of the many opportunities pupils must have in order to develop their knowledge of multiplication facts.

Preparation

During the main activity each pair will need a copy of photocopiable page 126 so you will need to make suffficient copies of these. Each pair will also need a special six-sided dice with faces labelled 'x 2', 'x 5' and 'x 10' (each label should appear on two faces). These can be produced using blank dice which are available from educational suppliers or you could adapt ordinary six-sided dice. If children carry out the extension and support activities you will need to supply them with an appropriately adapted number grid (see the extension and support activities opposite).

Resources

Photocopiable page 126, normal six-sided dice, special six-sided dice (see 'Preparation'), a supply of counters in two colours, calculators, paper, pencils. For the extension activity – appropriately adapted number grids. For the support activity – appropriately adapted dice and number grids.

What to do

Introduction

Start with some revision of multiplication facts involving 2s, 5s and 10s. This can be done in a variety of ways. The class could count in 2s, each child calling out one of the numbers in the sequence. Indicate who calls out the next number by pointing at a pupil. In this way you can point at the less able children near the beginning of the sequence and save the larger numbers for the more able. Keep a check on who has called out a number by telling everyone to put their hands on their heads at the start. When they

have called out a number they must take their hands off their heads. You could also use a stopwatch to time how long it takes to complete the sequence (every pupil must call out one number). Repeat this with 5s and 10s.

Another possibility is to use quick-fire questions, for example: *Three fives? Two times seven?* and so on. Again, match the questions to the ability of the pupils. You may like to use this as an opportunity to recap or introduce the language associated with multiplication such as 'times', 'multiplied by' and 'lots of'.

Main activity

Organize the children into pairs. Give each pair a copy of photocopiable page 126, a normal six-sided dice, an adapted six-sided dice, a supply of counters in two colours, a calculator and some paper. Explain that each child takes it in turns to roll the two dice. They must work out the answer to the resulting multiplication, say it (for example, 'four times five equals twenty'), look for the answer on the grid, and then cover it with a counter of their own colour. Disputes can be settled using the calculator. If an answer is incorrect then the counter is not placed on the grid. You might also want children to record their multiplications on paper. Explain that the objective is for each child to get three counters of their own colour next to each other in a line either horizontally, vertically or diagonally.

Plenary

Start by telling the children that you have deliberately included one number on the grid which is impossible to cover and ask them to work out which one it is (9, in the centre of the grid). Encourage the children to explain their answers and to provide you with other numbers which are not in the 2, 5 and 10 times tables (and therefore not on the grid). Follow this with questions such as: *Tell me a number which is in the 2 and the 5 times tables. Tell me a number which is in the 2s, 5s and 10s,* and so on.

You could also repeat the activities used during the introduction, again using a stopwatch to see how quickly the class can complete each sequence. Has the lesson improved their ability to recall multiples of 2, 5 and 10?

Suggestion(s) for extension

Children could use a ten or twelve-sided dice instead of the normal six-sided. This will generate additional answers so you will have to produce a suitable number grid for pupils to use.

Suggestion(s) for support

This activity should be accessible to the majority of children but one possible variation is to use a dice showing only 1, 2 and 3 (each number should be shown twice) instead of the normal six-sided dice. Children could also play a game which involves only doubling. They roll a six-sided dice, double the score and cover the answer on the grid. Similarly, they could play a game which involves only multiplication by 10. In all cases you will need to produce a grid containing appropriate numbers.

Assessment opportunities

By observing and listening to children throughout the lesson you will learn much about their developing knowledge of multiplication facts. If pupils record their multiplications during the main activity this will also provide useful evidence of their progress.

Reference to photocopiable sheet

Photocopiable page 126 displays a number grid. Using multiplication, children attempt to cover all the numbers on the grid. (You may be able to find other uses for the grid. See the activity 'Find...' on page 73, particularly the 'Suggestion(s) for extension' section.)

Multiplication practice

5	10	50	30	8	4	25
60	2	20	6	15	20	12
10	15	40	5	30	10	6
30	4	25	9	20	50	2
8	60	2	10	8	25	40
50	12	6	30	4	5	20
20	40	15	60	10	30	12

TWO COINS IN MY POCKET

To practise addition skills involving one and two-digit numbers in the context of money.

†† *Whole-class introduction followed by individual work and a whole-class plenary.*

🕐 *Introduction 5–10 minutes; main activity 15–20 minutes; plenary 10–15 minutes; total 30–45 minutes.*

Previous skills/knowledge needed

Children should have some experience of addition involving numbers beyond 10.

Key background information

It is important that children practise their addition facts and mental methods for addition in a wide range of situations. The activity described here is of an open-ended nature and uses money as a context to develop addition skills.

Preparation

Ensure that you have one of each of the coins currently in circulation so that you can show these to the children during the introduction.

Resources

Coins, pencils, paper, board/flip chart.

What to do

Introduction

Start by discussing the coins we use in our money system. Ask the children how many different coins are in common use, what the denominations are, what they look like, their size, their colour, and so on. Use actual examples to aid your discussions. You could ask pupils to arrange the coins in order according to size or denomination and use this as an opportunity to reinforce a wide range of appropriate language.

Main activity

Tell the children that you have got two coins in your pocket and ask them to guess how much money there could be altogether. Let several pupils provide answers but ensure they say what the two coins are as well as the total.

Working individually, pupils must then list all the possible amounts of money that could be in your pocket. They should continue to assume that you only have two coins in your pocket. Stress that they must record the values of the two coins as well as the total amount each time. This can be recorded in various ways according to the age and ability of pupils, ranging from informal ways such as:

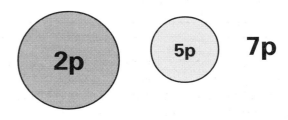

through to more formal ways such as:

$$2p + 5p = 7p$$

Check the children's lists to see whether any amounts are repeated. Point this out to them but let them work out for themselves which one has been repeated. Also, check the children's lists carefully when they think they have finished since there are likely to be some omissions. There should be 28 different amounts if seven coins are used (1p, 2p, 5p, 10p, 20p, 50p and £1) and 36 different amounts if you include the £2 coin.

Plenary

Work with the whole class to compile a list of all the possible amounts of money. Start by writing these on the board at random as the pupils call them out. Then stop and ask if anyone can think of a way of listing them so that none are missed out or written down twice. Hopefully, someone will suggest a logical, methodical approach. Otherwise you might have to suggest one yourself. Here is one possible way of setting it out.

1p + 1p = 2p						
1p + 2p = 3p	2p + 2p = 4p					
1p + 5p = 6p	2p + 5p = 7p	5p + 5p = 10p				
1p + 10p = 11p	2p + 10p = 12p	5p + 10p = 15p	10p + 10p = 20p			
1p + 20p = 21p	2p + 20p = 22p	5p + 20p = 25p	10p + 20p = 30p	20p + 20p = 40p		
1p + 50p = 51p	2p + 50p = 52p	5p + 50p = 55p	10p + 50p = 60p	20p + 50p = 70p	50p + 50p = £1	
1p + £1 = £1.01	2p + £1 = £1.02	5p + £1 = 1.05	10p + £1 = £1.10	20p + £1 = £1.20	50p + £1 = £1.50	£1 + £1 = £2

To further your own mathematical development you might like to compare the visual pattern above with the domino pattern shown on page 52. Can you see the connection between the way spots can be arranged on a set of dominoes and ways you can select two coins from a possible seven?

Suggestion(s) for extension
Ask children who complete the initial task to consider the possibility of you having three coins in your pocket, in the same way that they did with two.

Suggestion(s) for support
Some children may not be capable of dealing with large numbers and so you could restrict the number of coins they use by saying, for example, *There are two coins in my pocket but I haven't got any 50p or £1 coins.*

Assessment opportunities
The children's written work will provide valuable evidence of their ability to add one and two-digit numbers mentally and also their ability to work in a logical way.

Display ideas
A list of the possible amounts of money, organized in a logical way such as the example shown above, can be displayed in the classroom.

A BOOK OF STAMPS

To practise addition skills involving one and two-digit numbers in the context of money.

†† *Whole-class introduction followed by individual work and a whole-class plenary.*

🕐 *Introduction 5–10 minutes; main activity 15–20 minutes; plenary 10–15 minutes; total 30–45 minutes.*

Previous skills/knowledge needed
It is assumed that the children will have some experience of addition involving numbers beyond ten.

Key background information
This is another activity which provides pupils with an opportunity to practise their addition facts and develop their mental skills.

Preparation
Buy a book of stamps to show to pupils during the introduction. Try to use one which contains stamps of different denominations (books from stamp machines are usually of this type).

Resources
One book of stamps, paper, pencils, board/flip chart.

What to do

Introduction

Ask the children if they have ever seen a book of stamps and ask them to explain what it is, what it looks like, how many stamps it contained and so on. Hold up your book of stamps for the class to see and tell them the values of the stamps. Raise further questions such as: *Which stamp has the lowest value? Which one has the highest value?* and *What is the total value of the stamps?*

Draw this book of stamps on the board.

10p	5p
2p	1p

Ask pupils to tell you an amount of postage that can be made with these stamps, or ask a more direct question such as: *Can you make 16p of postage?* Let children provide several examples of postage that can be made using combinations of the four stamps.

Main activity

Hand out the paper and explain to the children that you want them to find as many different amounts of postage as possible which can be made with the four stamps shown above. Stress to pupils that they can use a single stamp, any two, any three or even all four stamps. The work can be recorded in various ways depending on the age and ability of the pupils. Some might use drawings of the stamps while others will use more formal notation. You could even provide a photocopied sheet of stamps in the four denominations shown above for pupils to cut out and stick onto paper.

Plenary

Ask the children to tell you the possible amounts of postage which can be made and summarize these on the board in a methodical way. Start with amounts using a single stamp, then amounts which use two stamps, then three stamps and finally all four stamps.

Four amounts can be made using a single stamp – 1p, 2p, 5p and 10p.
Six amounts can be made using two stamps – 3p, 6p, 7p, 11p, 12p and 15p.
Four amounts can be made using three stamps – 8p, 13p, 16p and 17p.
One amount can be made using all four stamps – 18p.

Now describe a slightly different situation. Ask children to imagine that they can use any number of 10p, 5p, 2p and 1p stamps. Ask them to explain how they could make

various amounts of postage, for example 50p, 13p, 34p, 26p. For each amount, ask pupils to explain different ways of doing it. The aim is to develop mental agility in adding numbers so it is important to maintain a lively pace during this part of the lesson.

Suggestion(s) for extension

Children do not have to use the same book of stamps. More able pupils could use a book which contains four stamps of higher denominations, or a book containing more than four stamps.

Suggestion(s) for support

It might be appropriate for some pupils to work with lower numbers, for example a book of four stamps with denominations 1p, 2p, 3p and 5p.

Assessment opportunities

The children's written work will provide evidence of their ability to add numbers. Also watch how individual pupils perform during the quick-fire practice sessions.

Display ideas

A list of possible amounts of postage, arranged in a logical way, could form the basis of a classroom display.

Handling data

During Key Stage One, pupils should be given opportunities to collect, use and make sense of a wide range of data which relates to their everyday experiences. The data should be real, meaningful and it must be collected for a purpose, rather than simply for the sake of it. The product of such work is usually tables, graphs and other diagrams. However, these can also be used to explore aspects of number as indicated in earlier sections of this book (for example block graphs are introduced in 'Odd and even with dominoes' on page 54).

Another important aspect of handling data at Key Stage One involves matching, pairing, sorting and classifying objects using various criteria. These could relate to the physical appearance of the objects, for example shape, size or colour, or to numerical properties. Several activities in earlier sections of this book touch on these skills, but they are not the main focus. However, in the case of the three activities described in this section, the ability to sort and classify is a key learning objective. This is achieved through practical activities in which both physical and numerical properties are considered.

SORTING WITH HOUSE CARDS

To identify similarities and differences in a set of objects. To sort a set of objects using a Carroll diagram.

†† *Whole-class introduction followed by work in pairs and a whole-class plenary.*

🕐 *Introduction 15–20 minutes; main activity 15–20 minutes; plenary 15–20 minutes; total 45–60 minutes.*

Previous skills/knowledge needed
Children should have some experience of early sorting and matching activities using a wide range of criteria.

Key background information
The ability to pair, match and sort lies at the heart of data-handling and also many aspects of number work. For example, children need to be able to pair a quantity or position with the corresponding number symbol (usually called number recognition), match numbers that have something in common (such as even numbers), and sort numbers into groups. These important skills and concepts, however, can be developed initially in non-numerical contexts. Children can identify red counters because they match and can then go on to sort a set of counters into two sets; those which are red and those which are not red. The sorting activities described in this activity are largely based on physical as opposed to numerical characteristics and children are introduced to Carroll diagrams which were first used by the author and mathematician Lewis Carroll.

Preparation
Make a set of 16 house cards by copying photocopiable pages 127 and 128 onto card and cutting them up. Ensure there is one set for each pair of children. Prepare two sets for yourself to use during the introduction. Colour the doors of one set blue and the other set red and then mix them up to form a set of 32 house cards. These can be laminated to make them more durable. Secure a large sheet of paper to the wall close to where the children will be gathered during the introduction. Ensure that it is low enough for the children to reach easily. Depending on how far the children get with the main activity, you may need to prepare another set of objects for pupils to use during the extension activity.

Resources
Sets of house cards (made using photocopiable pages 127 and 128, see 'Preparation') large sheets of paper (A3 or

larger), one very large sheet of paper, small pieces of card or paper to use as labels (about 2cm × 10 cm), Blu-Tack, pencils.

What to do

Introduction

Hand out the set of 32 house cards, one card per pupil. Ask one or two pupils to describe the house in their own words, using additional prompts as necessary, for example: *What shape are the windows? Does it have a chimney?* and so on. Arrange the pupils into pairs (and a three if there is an odd number) and ask them to compare house cards with one another. Ask individual pupils to explain which things are the same and which things are different, again providing prompts when necessary, for example: *Are the windows the same shape?* and *Are the doors the same colour?*

Draw a vertical line down the middle of the large sheet of paper to divide it in half. Explain to the children that they are going to sort the houses into two groups, one group on the left side of the paper and the other on the right. Invite suggestions as to how the houses could be sorted. Quickly make two labels corresponding to the two groups (for instance 'chimneys' and 'no chimneys') and stick these above the left and right sides of the large sheet of paper so that it looks like this.

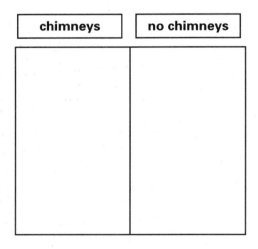

Ask pupils to come out, one at a time, and stick their houses on the appropriate side of the sheet using a small piece of Blu-Tack. Pick up on any errors and provide additional prompts as necessary.

Remove all of the house cards from the large sheet of paper and hand them out to the pupils again (you do not have to give them the same house cards that they had previously). Draw a horizontal line across the large sheet of paper so that it is now divided into quarters. Ask the children to suggest another way to sort the houses into two groups. Produce the corresponding labels (for example 'red doors' and 'blue doors') and stick these at the side of the large sheet of paper as shown in the next column.

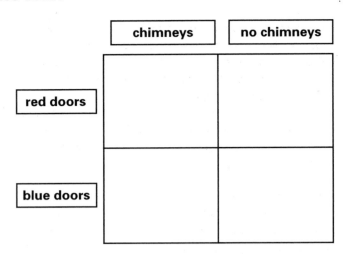

Ask one child to come to the front and use his or her house card as an example to explain the diagram. Use words such as 'right', 'left', 'top' and 'bottom' and reiterate these by pointing and using expressions such as 'above this line', 'below this line', 'this side of the line' and so on. Once you have demonstrated how the cards should be placed on the diagram, ask the children to come out again and stick their house cards in the appropriate section.

Try to use door colour as one of the criteria during the introduction because this is one which pupils will not be able to make use of during the main activity.

Main activity

Distribute one set of house cards, a large sheet of paper and some labels to each pair of pupils. Explain that they must first divide the sheet into two parts by drawing a vertical line. Then they must decide on the sorting criteria (just a single criteria to start with), produce two appropriate labels and then sort the houses into the two groups in the same way that they did during the introduction. Ask the children to use different sorting criteria to those used during the introduction.

When each pair has completed the initial task, check their work and then explain the next stage. They must remove the cards from the sheet, draw a horizontal line across the sheet, choose a second criteria, produce appropriate labels and finally sort the houses based on the two criteria.

Children who complete the second task can repeat it using two new criteria.

Plenary

Pick up on any common errors or misconceptions that have become apparent during the main activity. Then play the following game with the pupils using the house cards. Tell them that you have picked out one of the houses in your mind and they must try to work out which one it is. They must do this by asking questions to which you will only reply 'yes' or 'no'. See if they can think of a suitable question or alternatively provide an example for them such as *Does it have a red door?* Let one of the children ask the first question and then provide them with the appropriate response. Remove from the wall those houses which can be eliminated and explain this to the children (the set of 32 houses should still be on the wall from the introduction). Invite another question, provide a 'yes' or 'no' response, and then ask one of the pupils to come out and remove the houses which can be eliminated. See how many more questions are required to work out which house you have picked.

Suggestion(s) for extension

The activities described above can be carried out using another set of objects, for example mathematical shapes in different sizes, colours and thicknesses. Prepare sets of objects beforehand for some pupils to use if you think they will quickly complete the main activities and so need something more challenging.

Suggestion(s) for support

The main activities should be accessible to most pupils, although some might need additional support from you or another adult. It might also be appropriate for them to concentrate only on sorts which involve a single criteria.

Assessment opportunities

This activity produces no written evidence but you will learn much about the children's ability to work logically by observing them carefully throughout the session, particularly during the main activity. Firstly, watch to see whether the children can identify their own sorting criteria since this demonstrates an awareness of similarities and differences in the house cards. Secondly, observe their ability to actually sort the house cards using the chosen criteria.

Display ideas

The large sheet of paper and set of 32 house cards can be used as an interactive display. At the start of each day, two children can be given the responsibility of choosing criteria and then carrying out the sort. You could remove the cards and labels at the end of each day ready for the next morning.

Reference to photocopiable sheets

Photocopiable pages 127 and 128 each display eight houses with slight variations. These are used by the children to carry out various sorting activities.

MULTILINK HOUSES

To investigate the number of ways in which objects can be arranged. To classify objects using a sorting diagram.

†† *Whole-class introduction followed by individual work and a whole-class plenary.*

🕐 *Introduction 5–10 minutes; main activity 15–20 minutes; plenary 15–20 minutes; total 35–50 minutes.*

Previous skills/knowledge needed

It is assumed that children are familiar with the concept of sorting using pictorial methods such as a Carroll diagram.

Key background information

During Key Stage One, children should be given the opportunity to work through investigative activities in which they are required to find how many ways a particular task can be completed. This helps them to appreciate that there are often several possible answers to a problem and encourages them to compare the possibilities to see whether they are the same or different. This could involve number (*How many ways can you make 10?*), money (*How many ways can you make first class postage using these four stamps?*) or physical objects (*How many ways can these three books be arranged on a shelf?*). These activities are suitable for all ages and abilities because at the lowest level they can be tackled using simple trial and improvement methods while more able pupils can use

more methodical approaches. Eventually this could lead to the identification of patterns, and the making of predictions and generalizations. In the activity described below, children are asked to investigate colour combinations using multilink cubes, and then classify them using a diagram which should highlight the patterns in the results.

Preparation

Ensure you have a large quantity of multilink cubes and ideally multilink prisms as well, although it is possible to do the activity without the latter. Draw the two labelled grids shown in the plenary section opposite on two large sheets of paper.

Resources

Multilink cubes and prisms, plain or 2cm squared paper, coloured pencils or crayons, labelled grids.

What to do

Introduction

Clip together a red multilink cube and a red prism to form a 'house'. Explain to the children that in 'Multilink Town' the houses are always made from one cube and one prism. (If you do not have prisms then clip together two red cubes and explain that the houses are always made out of two cubes, one for upstairs and one for downstairs.) At the front of the class have a pile of red cubes and prisms and a pile of blue cubes and prisms (or just cubes if you have no prisms). Explain to the children that you only have reds

and blues and then ask them to describe a house that you could make – for example, using a red cube and a blue prism, a blue cube and a blue prism. Let one of the pupils make the house they describe and hold it up for everyone to see. Ask for another example and allow another child to make it.

Now introduce a third pile of cubes and prisms in a different colour, for example white. Ask the children to describe a house which could be made now that you have got three colours to choose from. Stress that a house still comprises one cube and one prism (or two cubes). Let a pupil make another house and hold it up. Ask for a second example choosing from the three colours.

Main activity

Tell the children that they must choose two colours of multilink and make as many different houses as they can. These can be recorded on plain or 2cm squared paper using coloured pencils or crayons in the appropriate colours. Again, stress that a house comprises one cube and one prism (or two cubes).

When individual children have completed the initial task, check their houses. There should be four: red-red, red-blue, blue-red and blue-blue. Then tell them to choose a third colour and see how many different houses they can make now. Again these can be recorded on 2cm squared paper (there should be nine different houses).

Plenary

Start by asking pupils how many different houses they managed to make when they used just two colours. Most, if not all pupils should give the correct answer. Then say that you are all going to check to see whether this is correct. Attach a large sheet of paper to the wall showing this grid.

roof colour

	red	blue
red		
blue		

house colour

Note: If you are using only cubes then the labels should read 'upstairs colour' and 'downstairs colour'.

roof colour

	red	blue	white
red			
blue			
white			

house colour

Note: If you are using only cubes then the labels should read 'upstairs colour' and 'downstairs colour'.

Let one of the children quickly make a house using only reds and blues and ask them in which part of the diagram it belongs. Discuss and explain this to the class if necessary. Quickly draw the house in the appropriate part of the diagram or let the pupil draw it. Repeat this until all four houses have been drawn, one in each part of the diagram.

Then introduce a third colour, for example white, and ask the children how many different houses can be made. Point to the diagram you have just been using and pose questions such as: *Could we draw the houses on this diagram? Where would we put a house which is all white? How must we change this diagram?* and so on. By asking the right sorts of questions, and providing appropriate prompts, you should be able to get the children to describe the 3 × 3 grid shown above.

Attach the grid you prepared earlier to the wall. Ask a child to make a house and hold it in the appropriate part of the diagram. Explain and discuss as necessary while the pupil draws the house on the grid. Repeat this until all nine houses have been drawn on the grid, one in each part of the diagram.

Finally, ask the children what the grid would look like if you were making houses using four colours. See whether, based on their experience of the earlier grids, they can work out how many different houses there would be and also explain their answers.

Suggestion(s) for extension

The main activity should provide sufficient challenge for most pupils but if necessary you could ask children who require extension work to find all the different houses using four colours.

Suggestion(s) for support

The nature of the main activity should make it accessible to all pupils in the class, although some may benefit from adult assistance.

Assessment opportunities

During the main activity watch how pupils tackle the problem. Some will make houses at random while others will make and record them in a more systematic way. If you see a child adopting this sort of approach ask him or her to explain what they are doing and why they are doing it that way. Similarly, when pupils say they have made all of the possible houses, ask them how they know they have not missed any out. Your observations and pupils' responses will provide an insight into their ability to think logically.

Display ideas

The diagrams produced during the plenary would make an excellent display.

SORTING WITH DOMINOES

To sort a set of dominoes according to the numbers of spots. To apply knowledge of odd and even numbers. To understand the relationship between odd and even numbers when they are added.

†† *Whole-class introduction followed by work in pairs and a whole-class plenary.*

⏱ *Introduction 10–15 minutes; main activity 20–25 minutes; plenary 15–20 minutes; total 45–60 minutes.*

Previous skills/knowledge needed

Pupils will need to be familiar with odd and even numbers and have some experience of sorting using a Carroll diagram or something similar.

Key background information

This activity pulls together two strands covered earlier in this book; odd and even numbers using dominoes (see the activity 'Odd and even with dominoes' on page 54) and sorting with a Carroll diagram (see 'Sorting with house cards' on page 85). In this activity pupils are given the opportunity to apply their existing knowledge and understanding in order to investigate what happens when odd and even numbers are added together. The activity is presented in such a way that children should be able to spot the patterns and relationships that exist.

Preparation

Ensure that you have sufficient sets of dominoes to allow one set for each pair of pupils. Use photocopiable page 118 to make sets from card or paper if necessary. Use the sheet to make one set of paper or card dominoes to use during the introduction and plenary.

Resources

Each pair of pupils will need a set of dominoes, two large sheets of paper (A3 or larger) and pencils. You will need one very large sheet of paper, a set of paper or card dominoes and some Blu-Tack.

What to do

Introduction

If the pupils have not used dominoes before then introduce this new resource by asking questions such as: *What does a domino look like? Which domino has the most spots? Which one has the fewest? How many dominoes have six spots on one half?* and so on. Use actual dominoes to demonstrate answers and assist explanations.

Then discuss odd and even numbers by considering each half of a domino separately rather than the total number of spots. Ask pupils to give examples of dominoes which have odd numbers of spots on both halves, even numbers on both halves and finally one odd and one even on each half. Display a large sheet of paper on the wall and divide it into three labelled parts as shown below.

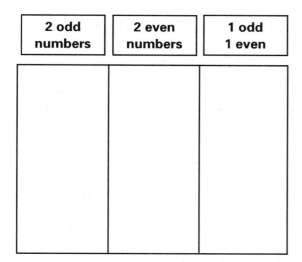

2 odd numbers	2 even numbers	1 odd 1 even

Hold up one of the paper or card dominoes which you have prepared earlier and ask pupils whether the numbers on each half are odd or even. Ask one of the pupils to stick the domino in the appropriate part of the diagram using Blu-Tack. Repeat this with one or two other dominoes. One important issue which needs to be discussed is whether zero (a blank half) is odd or even. Pupils may well raise this themselves during your discussions. Respond initially by asking the class what they think. Then explain it in terms of sequences or the way that odd and even numbers alternate as we count forwards or backwards. Reach the conclusion that we should consider zero to be even, at least in this particular activity.

Before explaining the main activity, ask pupils which part of the diagram they think will contain the most dominoes if a complete set were sorted. They are about to find out for themselves.

Main activity

Organize the children into pairs. Give each pair a large sheet of paper and ask them to divide them into three labelled regions and arrange the set of dominoes appropriately (as you demonstrated to them earlier). When the dominoes have been sorted, pupils can record their work by drawing each domino on the sheet. There should be 6 dominoes in the odd-odd region, 10 in the even-even region and 12 in the odd-even region.

Give those who complete the initial task a fresh sheet of paper. Tell them to divide this into six regions by drawing two vertical lines and one horizontal line. Explain to pupils that the left, middle and right parts of the sheets are for odd-odd, even-even and odd-even dominoes respectively, just like before. The top and bottom parts of the diagram

are for odds and evens respectively when the total number of spots on each domino are counted. The labelled diagram should look like this.

	2 odd numbers	2 even numbers	1 odd 1 even
odd total			
even total			

Children must sort their set of dominoes using the diagram and then record their work just like before. You could explain the diagram to pairs or small groups of pupils as they finish the initial task. Alternatively, you could stop the whole class, gather them around your large sheet of paper displayed on the wall and explain it to them in the same way as you did during the introduction.

Plenary

Start by asking which of the three initial regions (odd-odd, even-even, and odd-even) had the most dominoes in it. Is this what the pupils had previously anticipated?

Next, divide your large sheet of paper into six regions and label them as shown on the previous page. Hand out your set of 28 paper or card dominoes to the pupils and ask them to come out, one at a time, and stick their domino in the appropriate part of the diagram. Pick up on any errors or misconceptions and provide additional prompts and explanations as necessary.

All of the odd-odd and the even-even dominoes should be in the bottom half (have an even total) and all of the odd-even dominoes should be in the top half (have an odd total). Discuss this arrangement with the pupils. Ask questions such as: *Why are all of the odd-odd dominoes at the bottom? What does this mean about odd numbers when we add them together? Why are all of the even-even dominoes at the bottom? What does this mean about even numbers when we add them together? What happens when we add an odd number and an even number?* and so on.

Establish rules for adding pairs of odd and even numbers and ask the children whether they think these rules work for all numbers or only apply to dominoes. Use numbers beyond six to pose further questions and provide additional examples and explanations.

Suggestions for extension
The two stages of the main activity should pose a challenge for most pupils but in addition you could ask them to write down an explanation of the domino arrangement in their own words.

Suggestion(s) for support
The first stage of the main activity should be accessible to even the weakest pupils in the class.

Assessment opportunities
The children's written work will provide evidence of their knowledge of odd and even numbers and their ability to use a sorting diagram. You will also see evidence of this

during the introduction and plenary. Those pupils who are able to identify, explain and generalize the relationship between odd and even numbers, either in their writing or during the plenary, are showing high levels of achievement.

Display ideas
The completed sorting diagrams produced during this activity would make a valuable and attractive display.

Reference to photocopiable sheet
Make your own sets of dominoes using photocopiable page 118. Copy each set onto a different coloured piece of card to avoid the sets getting mixed up.

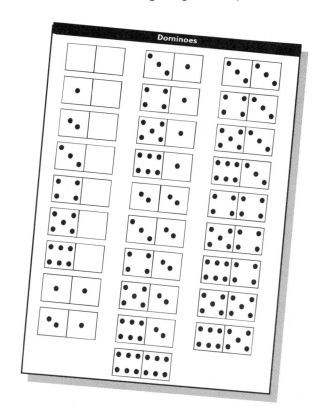

Calculator light-sticks, see page 15; Six light-sticks, see page 17

Calculator light-sticks

Name _____   Date _____

FURTHER *Curriculum Bank* ACTIVITIES
PHOTOCOPIABLES

Calculator fishing

Squeeze, see page 22

Squeeze

Name _____ Date _____

First roll	Squeeze	Second roll

Boxes, see page 24

Boxes

P		HIGH		P
L				L
A				A
Y				Y
E				E
R				R
O				T
N				W
E		LOW		O

Place value with HTU cards, see page 27; Addition with HTU cards, see page 69

Place value cards

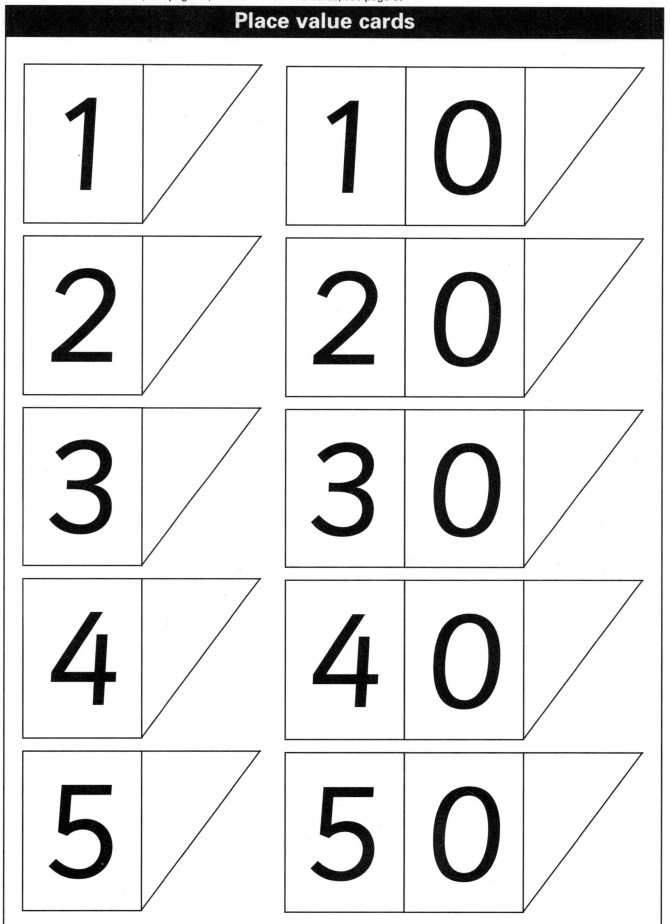

Place value cards

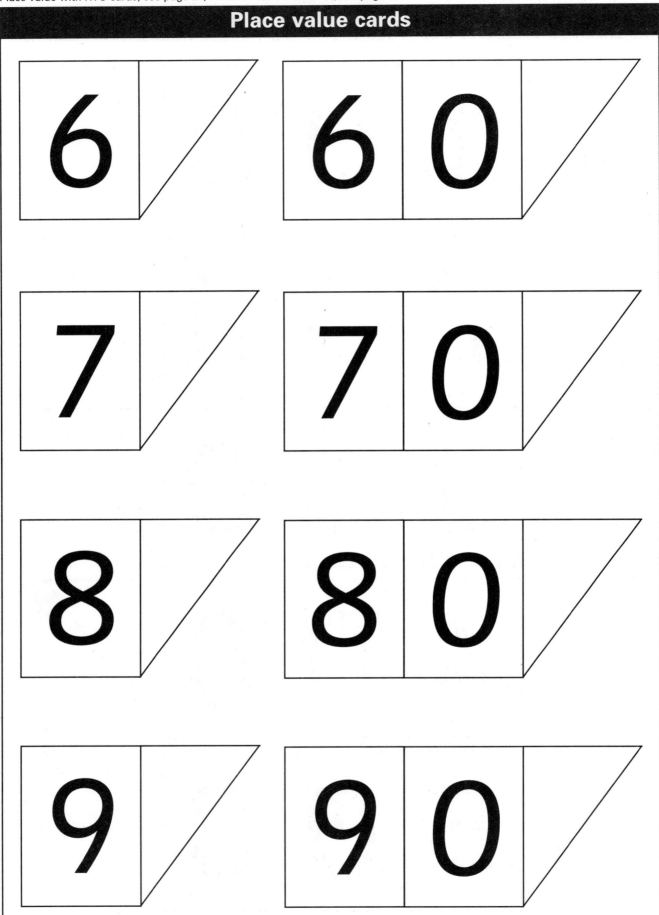

Place value with HTU cards, see page 27; Addition with HTU cards, see page 69

Place value cards

100

200

300

400

500

Place value with HTU cards, see page 27; Addition with HTU cards, see page 69

Place value cards

6	0	0

7	0	0

8	0	0

9	0	0

Place value with HTU cards, see page 27; Addition with HTU cards, see page 69

Place value with HTU cards, see page 27

Place value cards recording sheet

Name _____   Date _____

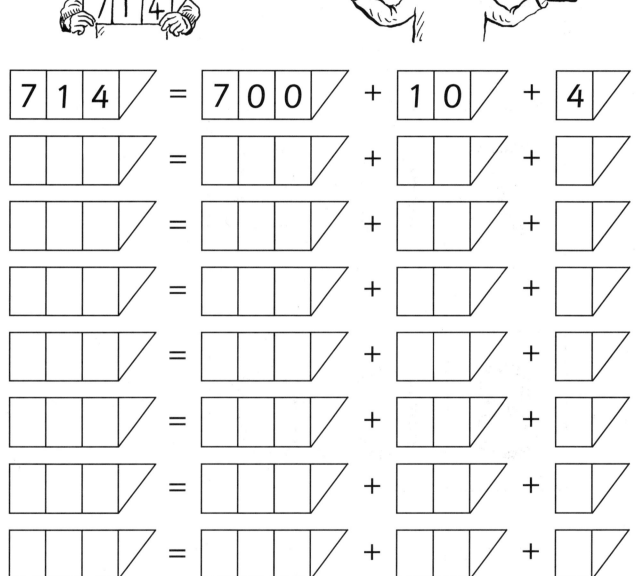

| 7 1 4 | = | 7 0 0 | + | 1 0 | + | 4 |

Place value with HTU cards, see page 27

Place value cards recording sheet

Name _____ Date _____

| 3 8 | = | 3 0 | + | 8 |

Making numbers, see page 29

Digit cards

0	1	2
3	4	5
6	7	8
	9	

Number flip-flaps, see page 31

Number flip-flap

1	5	7	6
9			8
4			3
8	2	1	0

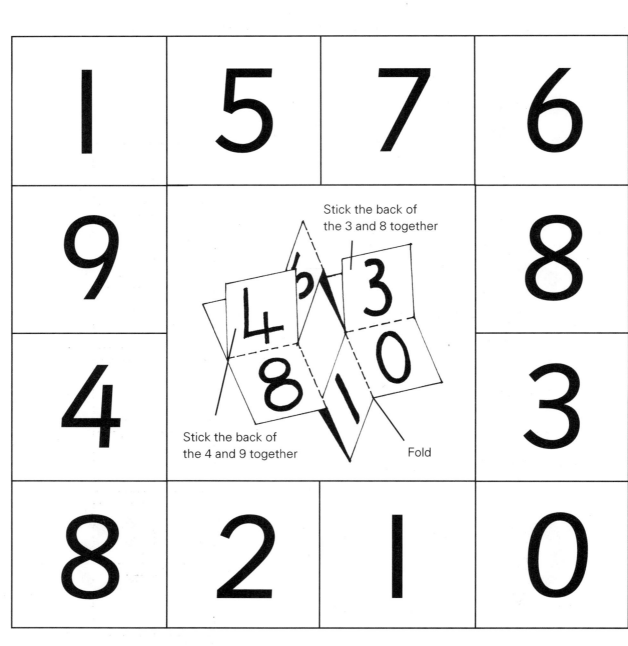

Stick the back of
the 3 and 8 together

Stick the back of
the 4 and 9 together

Fold

FURTHER *Curriculum Bank* ACTIVITIES
PHOTOCOPIABLES

Number flip-flap recording sheet

Name _____ Date _____

Use your number flip-flap to make

a number less than 20

a number between 20 and 30

a number between 30 and 40

a number between 40 and 50

a number between 50 and 60

a number between 60 and 70

a number between 70 and 80

a number between 80 and 90

a number between 90 and 100

Try to make as many two digit numbers as you can.

Place value dice games, see page 32

Dice games recording sheet

Name _____   Date _____

	Player One	Player Two
Game 1		
Game 2		
Game 3		
Game 4		
Game 5		
Game 6		
Game 7		
Game 8		
Game 9		
Game 10		

Fractions with pattern blocks, see page 35

Fractions with pattern blocks

Name _____ Date _____

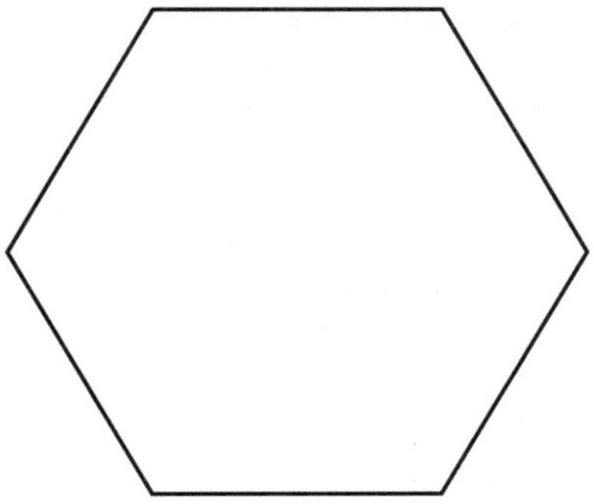

Half red

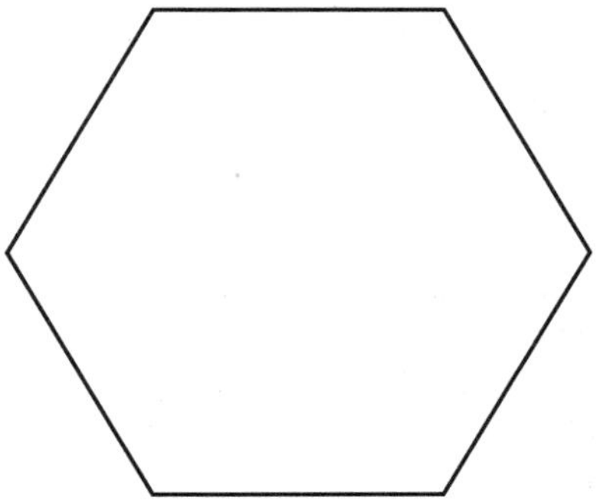

More than
half blue

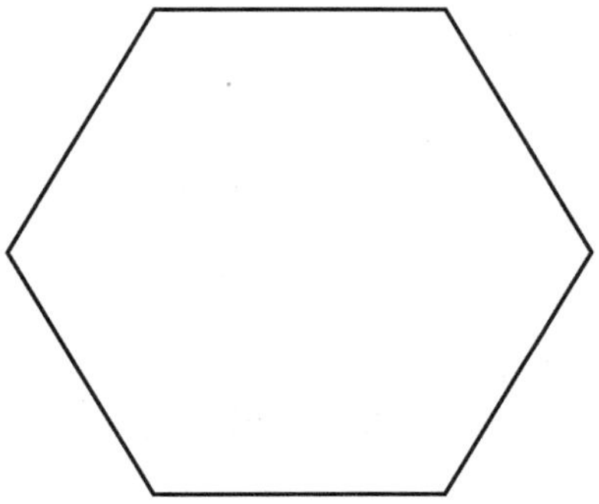

Less than
half blue

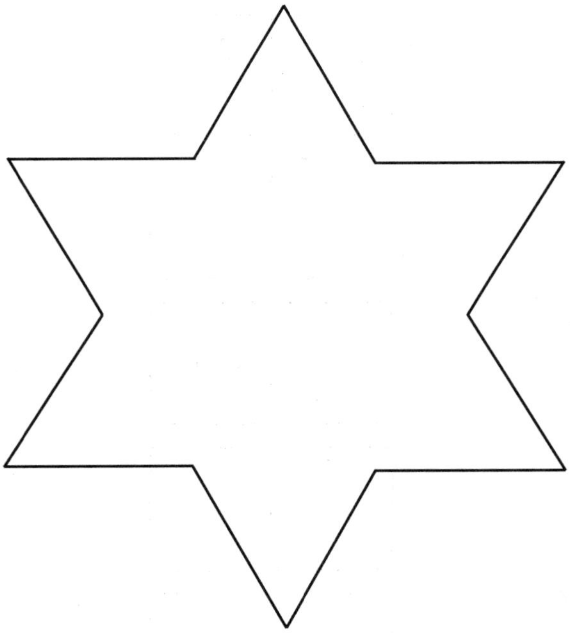

Half yellow

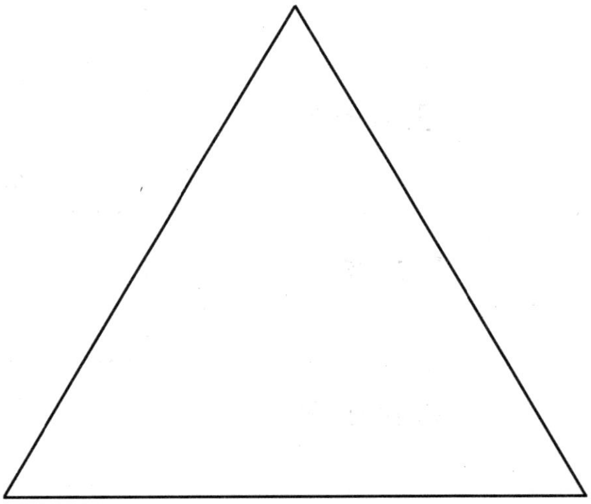

More than
half yellow

Fractions with pattern blocks, see page 35

Fractions with pattern blocks

Name _____   Date _____

More than half red

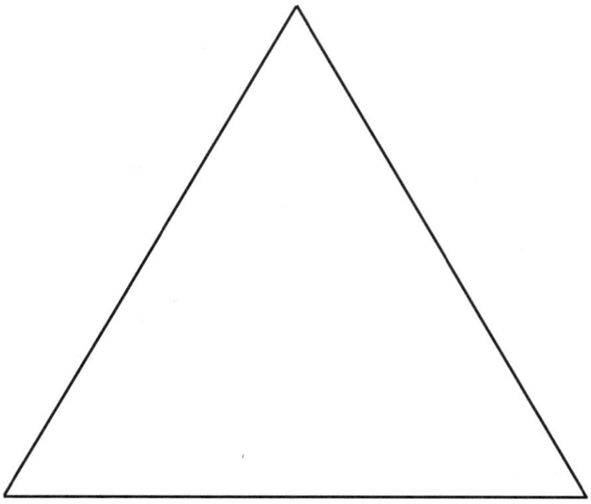

Less than
half red

Half blue

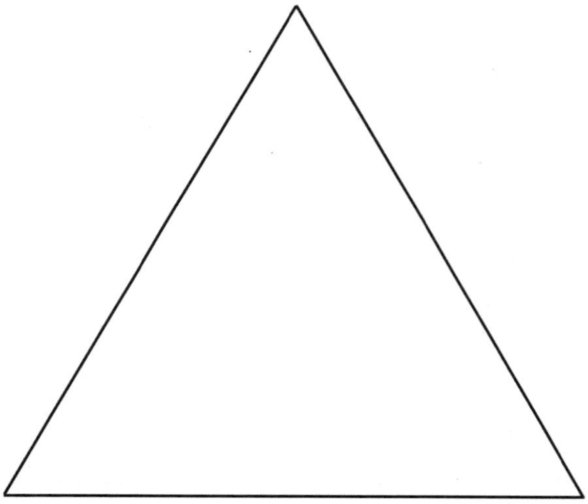

Less than
half blue

Fractions with pattern blocks, see page 35

Fractions with pattern blocks

Name _____   Date _____

Half red

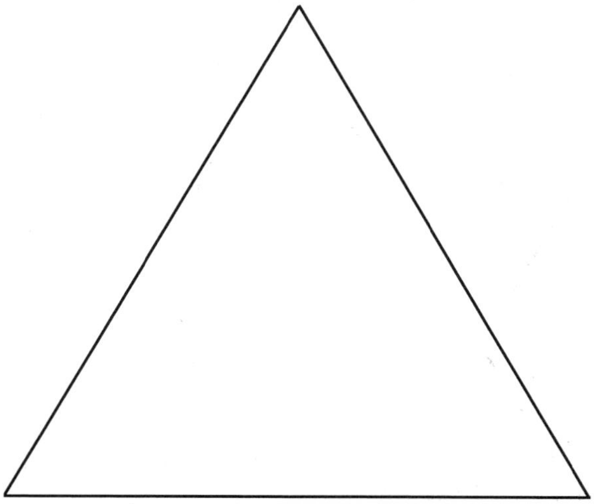

More than
half red

Less than half green

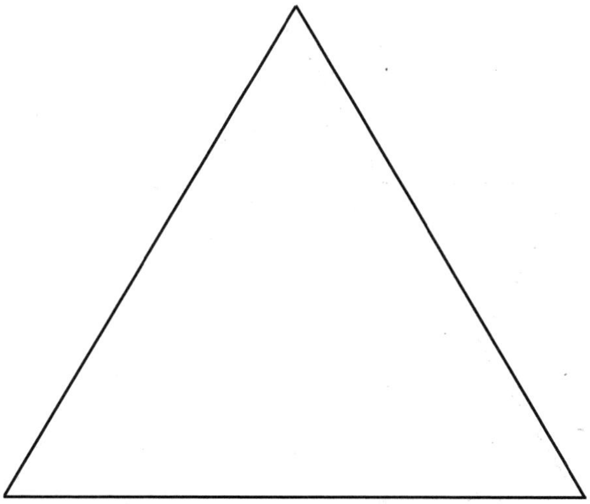

Half green

100-square jigsaws, see page 40

Jigsaw pieces

Jigsaw pieces

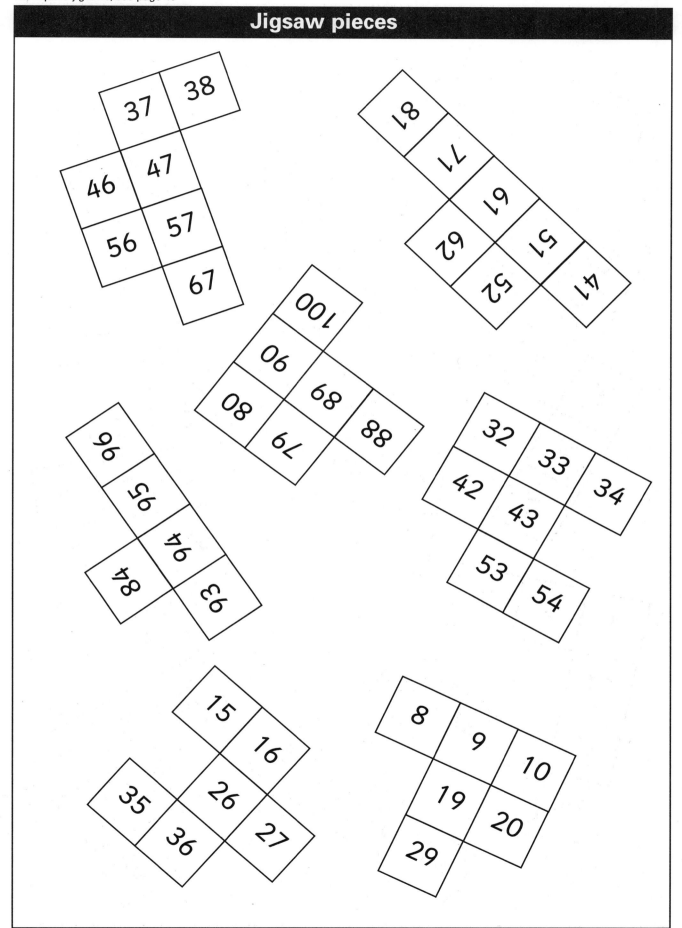

100-square jigsaws, see page 40

Jigsaw grid

1	2	3	4	5	6	7	8	9	10
11	12	13	14	15	16	17	18	19	20
21	22	23	24	25	26	27	28	29	30
31	32	33	34	35	36	37	38	39	40
41	42	43	44	45	46	47	48	49	50
51	52	53	54	55	56	57	58	59	60
61	62	63	64	65	66	67	68	69	70
71	72	73	74	75	76	77	78	79	80
81	82	83	84	85	86	87	88	89	90
91	92	93	94	95	96	97	98	99	100

Number necklaces, see page 41

Number necklaces

Name _____   Date _____

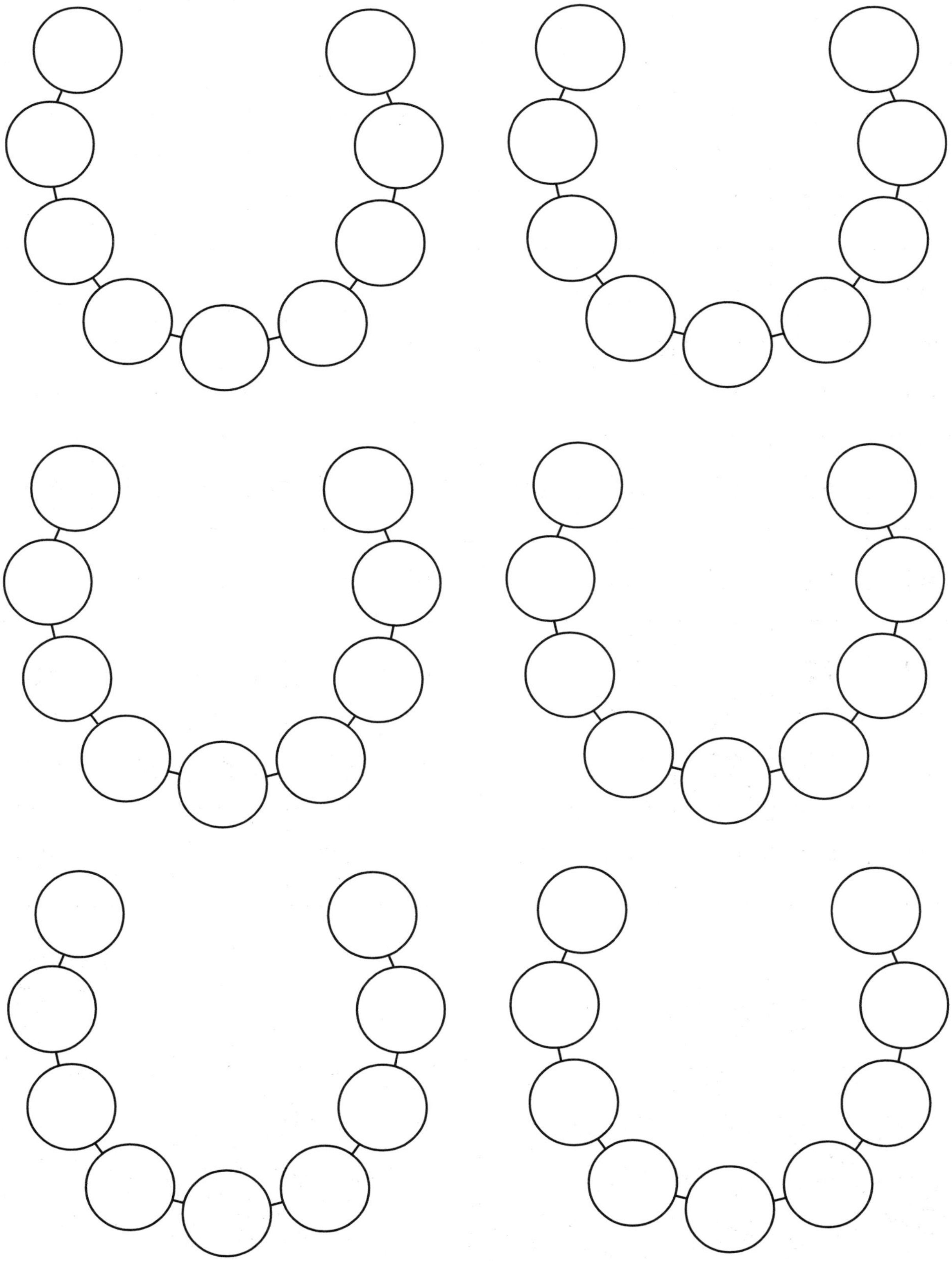

Shading patterns, see page 43

Shading patterns

Name _____   Date _____

1	2	3	4	5	6	7	8	9	10
11	12	13	14	15	16	17	18	19	20
21	22	23	24	25	26	27	28	29	30
31	32	33	34	35	36	37	38	39	40
41	42	43	44	45	46	47	48	49	50

1	2	3	4	5	6	7	8	9	10
11	12	13	14	15	16	17	18	19	20
21	22	23	24	25	26	27	28	29	30
31	32	33	34	35	36	37	38	39	40
41	42	43	44	45	46	47	48	49	50

Shading patterns, see page 43

Shading patterns

1	2	3	4	5	6	7	8	9	10	11	12
13	14	15	16	17	18	19	20	21	22	23	24
25	26	27	28	29	30	31	32	33	34	35	36
37	38	39	40	41	42	43	44	45	46	47	48

1	2	3	4	5	6	7	8
9	10	11	12	13	14	15	16
17	18	19	20	21	22	23	24
25	26	27	28	29	30	31	32
33	34	35	36	37	38	39	40

1	2	3	4	5
6	7	8	9	10
11	12	13	14	15
16	17	18	19	20
21	22	23	24	25
26	27	28	29	30

1	2	3	4	5	6	7	8	9	10	11
12	13	14	15	16	17	18	19	20	21	22
23	24	25	26	27	28	29	30	31	32	33
34	35	36	37	38	39	40	41	42	43	44

Stars and shapes, see page 46

Stars and shapes

Name _____   Date _____

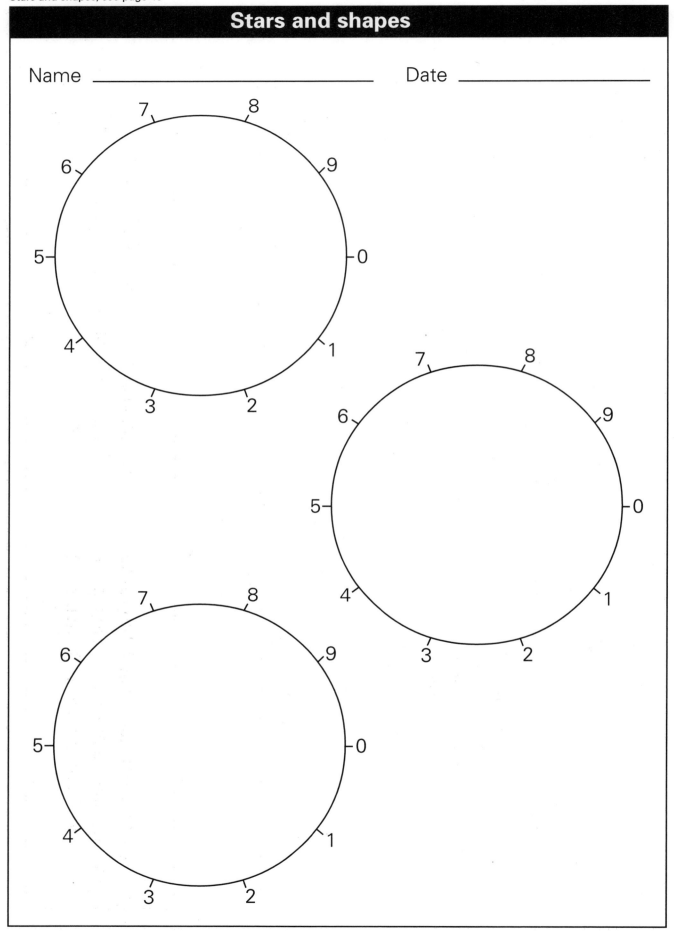

NUMBER KEY STAGE ONE

Dotty sequences, see page 48

Dot-to-dot

Name _____   Date _____

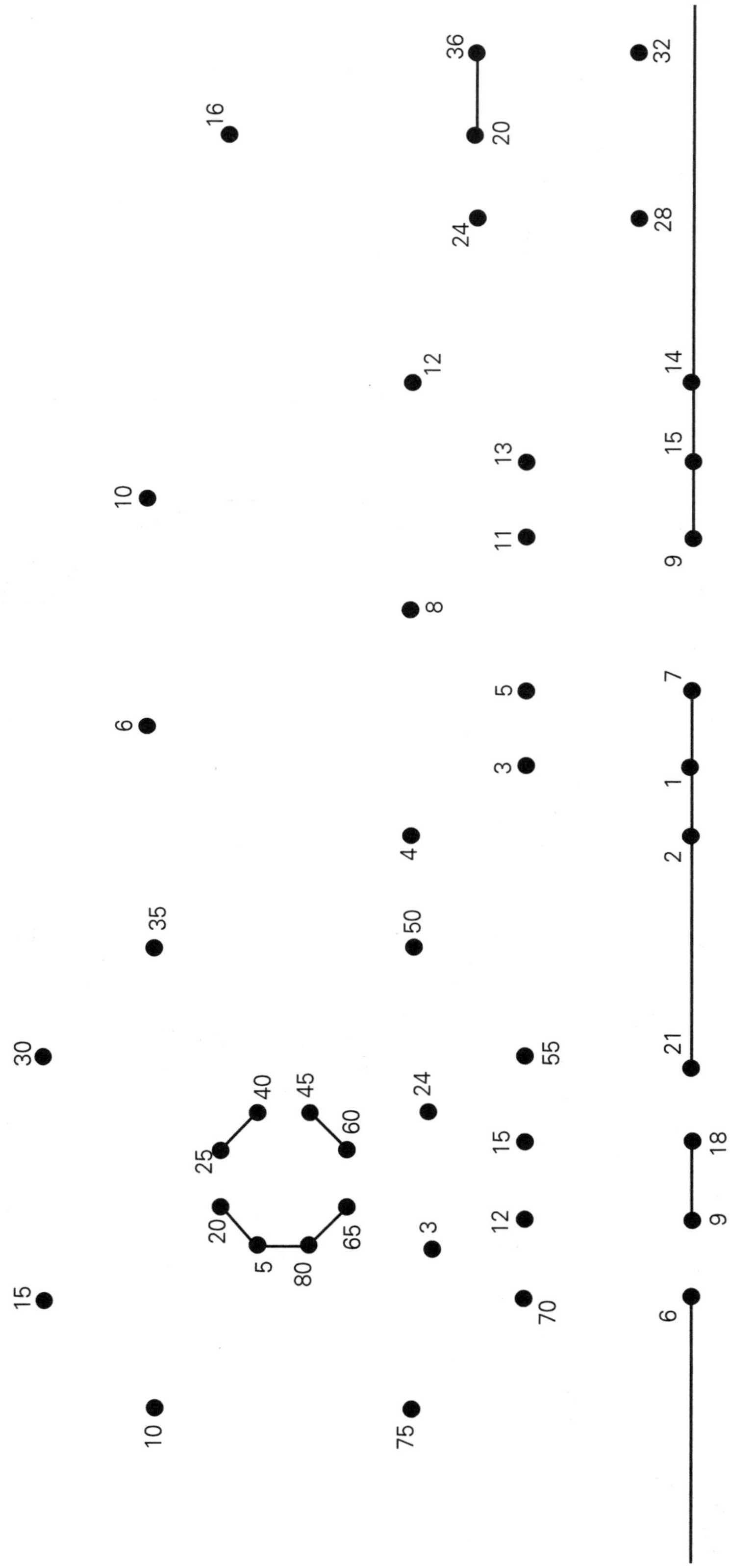

Counting in 4s starting at 4. Stop at 36.
Counting in 5s starting at 5. Stop at 80.

Even numbers starting at 2. Stop at 14.
Odd numbers starting at 1. Stop at 15.
Counting in 3s starting at 3. Stop at 24.

Hunt the domino, see page 52; also see the activities on pages 54, 60, 63, 65 and 90

Dominoes

Sets and sequences, see page 58

Sets and sequences

The five smallest numbers	The five biggest numbers
Numbers less than 12	Numbers between 5 and 15
Numbers between 20 and 30	Numbers between 34 and 43
Odd numbers up to 21	Even numbers up to 20
Odd numbers between 35 and 45	Even numbers from 70 to 80
The five biggest odd numbers	The five biggest even numbers
Counting in 5s up to 25	Counting in 10s up to 100
Counting in 5s from 50 to 100	Counting in 3s up to 30
Counting in 4s up to 40	Pairs of numbers that add up to 10
Counting in 10s starting at 5	Counting in 10s starting at 3
Counting in 5s starting at 2. Stop at 52.	Counting in 4s starting at 1. Stop at 45.
Counting in 3s starting at 2. Stop at 50.	Groups of three numbers that add up to 25
Multiples of 6	Multiples of 7
Multiples of 8	Multiples of 9

Domino squares

Name _____   Date _____

<table>
<tr><td></td><td>5</td><td></td><td>3</td></tr>
<tr><td></td><td>2</td><td></td><td>4</td></tr>
</table>

    5   2   2   5

<table>
<tr><td></td><td>9</td><td></td><td>9</td></tr>
<tr><td></td><td>4</td><td></td><td>7</td></tr>
</table>

    6   7   8   8

<table>
<tr><td></td><td>10</td><td></td><td>12</td></tr>
<tr><td></td><td>9</td><td></td><td>1</td></tr>
</table>

    8   11   7   6

<table>
<tr><td></td><td>9</td></tr>
<tr><td></td><td>6</td></tr>
</table>

    11   4

NUMBER KEY STAGE ONE

Domino squares

Name _____ Date _____

| | 4 |
| | 3 |

2   5

| | 4 |
| | 7 |

6   5

| | 4 |
| | 7 |

4   7

| | 6 |
| | 7 |

9   4

| | 8 |
| | 2 |

6   4

| | 11 |
| | 5 |

6   10

| | 6 |
| | 4 |

0   10

Three in a row, see page 68; Find..., see page 73

Three in a row

9	13	20	5	2	14	6
1	16	4	6	18	10	15
12	7	10	17	5	3	8
6	15	0	8	12	7	13
3	2	11	2	4	1	16
14	8	10	20	9	15	11
18	12	4	19	17	10	5

Arithmetic search, see page 72

Arithmetic search

Name _____   Date _____

2	+	5	=	7	3	+	3	=	6
9	8	–	3	=	5	+	4	=	9
+	+	4	+	6	=	10	+	7	=
1	3	=	2	+	1	+	5	=	8
=	=	1	=	1	+	3	+	3	+
10	11	=	5	+	4	+	1	+	1
–	–	0	–	9	–	5	=	4	+
4	4	+	3	+	3	=	10	+	3
=	=	1	=	6	=	8	–	2	=
6	7	=	2	+	5	+	5	=	12

Find...

1. Find two numbers next to each other that
add up to 5
add up to 10
add up to 15
add up to 20
add up to 25
add up to 30

2. Find three numbers next to each other in a line that
add up to 15
add up to 20
add up to 25
add up to 30
add up to 35
add up to 40

3. Find four numbers next to each other in a line that
add up to 25
add up to 30
add up to 35
add up to 40
add up to 45
add up to 50
add up to 55

4. Find four numbers that form a square and
add up to 35
add up to 40
add up to 45
add up to 65

Doubling three-in-a-row

1	10	6	5	2	3	6
4	8	2	4	10	8	4
2	3	12	6	1	2	10
6	1	5	7	3	6	4
2	4	10	2	8	5	12
6	12	8	6	4	1	2
5	4	3	12	2	6	4

Multiplication practice, see page 80

Multiplication practice

5	10	50	30	8	4	25
60	2	20	6	15	20	12
10	15	40	5	30	10	6
30	4	25	9	20	50	2
8	60	2	10	8	25	40
50	12	6	30	4	5	20
20	40	15	60	10	30	12

Sorting with house cards, see page 85

Houses

Sorting with house cards, see page 85

Houses